NURTURING CHILDREN & YOUTH THROUGH TRAUMA & COMPLEX CHALLENGES

HEALING GROWING HEARTS

Integrating Western, Indigenous, And Afrocentric Approaches For Transformative Healing

ESEOSA OMOREGIE

Copyright © 2025, Eseosa Omoregie
All Rights Reserved.

No part of this publication may be reproduced, stored in a retrieval system, or transmitted in any form or by any means—electronic, mechanical, photocopying, recording, or others—except for brief quotations in critical reviews or articles, without the prior written permission of the author.

The right of Eseosa Omoregie to be identified as the author of this book has been asserted by her, in accordance with the copyright laws.

Independently published by: Eseosa Omoregie

For permissions, inquiries, and bulk purchase requests, kindly send an email to omoregieeseosa28@gmail.com

DEDICATION

This book is dedicated to every survivor of childhood and youth trauma—those still healing, those who have found their voice, and those just beginning to rediscover their strength. This is for you. You are not alone. May these words bring light to your path, and power to your story.

ACKNOWLEDGMENTS

Writing and publishing this book has been one of the most transformative journeys of my life, and I would be remiss not to acknowledge the many hearts and hands that carried me through it.

First and foremost, I thank **God**, who is the source of all inspiration, for planting the seed of this idea in my spirit and giving me the courage to nurture it into being.

To my parents, whom I love deeply, thank you for your unwavering support and for giving me the freedom to explore, learn, and grow. Your belief in me is the foundation of this work.

To my beautiful three-year-old son, **Jidenna**—your innocence, imagination, and unconditional love have been my daily motivation. Seeing the world through your bright eyes reminded me why healing matters.

To the many **researchers, social workers, and trauma-informed practitioners** who helped shape this book—your dedication and expertise were instrumental. A special thank you to Esther, a social worker whose insights deeply influenced this work.

To every **brave survivor** and **client** who trusted me enough to share their stories: your honesty and courage are the soul of this book. I hold your words with the utmost respect and gratitude.

To my **editor**, thank you for taking the raw vision in my mind and refining it into something powerful and clear. You helped me turn an idea into a book, and for that I am forever grateful.

To my **partner**, your love, kindness, and quiet strength were the anchor I didn't know I needed. Thank you for walking beside me in every chapter of this journey.

Finally, to **every single person, channel**, and **platform** that helped amplify the message of this book—thank you for sharing your energy and space. Your support helped bring this message into the world, where it can serve and heal.

With deep gratitude,
Eseosa Omoregie

DISCLOSURE STATEMENT

Some stories in this book are fictionalized accounts inspired by years of professional experience in the field. These fictional narratives are designed to reflect common themes, challenges, and healing journeys encountered in practice, while protecting the privacy of all individuals.

Stories that are not fictionalized have been included with the full, informed consent of the individuals involved. In all such cases, names and identifying details have been changed to uphold confidentiality and respect privacy.

This work may also include research, case studies, or stories drawn from publicly available sources, including published reports, academic studies, and open-access materials. Any resemblance to actual persons, living or deceased, is **purely coincidental,** unless explicitly stated with consent.

This content is shared in the spirit of healing, education, and advocacy, and all reasonable efforts have been made to ensure that it honors the dignity and privacy of those whose experiences have informed it.

PEER REVIEWS

"Healing Growing Hearts is a deeply compassionate and insightful book that shines a much-needed light on the emotional and psychological struggles faced by children and youth living through trauma. Thoughtfully organized into ten chapters, this book takes a comprehensive and trauma-informed approach to understanding and supporting young people in various challenging life circumstances.

Each chapter addresses a specific type of trauma—ranging from sexual abuse and exploitation to grief, parental estrangement, codependency, foster care, disability, displacement, and growing up in environments impacted by crime or military presence. What makes this book especially impactful is the incorporation of real-life stories from individuals who have lived through these experiences. These authentic voices not only validate the emotional realities of trauma survivors but also make the content practical, relatable, and humanizing.

The author skillfully defines key concepts and identifies different types of trauma and their effects, making complex psychological themes accessible to a wide audience. The inclusion of diverse cultural perspectives, particularly from Indigenous and Black/Black American communities, enriches the narrative by highlighting the layered and intergenerational nature of trauma in marginalized populations. These perspectives are too often overlooked in mainstream mental health literature, and their inclusion here offers an important corrective.

What stands out most in Healing Growing Hearts is its focus on healing—not just survival. Each chapter doesn't just explore the pain but offers pathways forward through practical strategies, affirming language, and culturally grounded support systems. The book emphasizes that healing is not linear and not the same for everyone, but it is always possible.

This is not just a book for therapists or social workers—though it would be invaluable for them—it's also a powerful resource for caregivers, educators, foster parents, and community members who want to better understand and support the children and youth in their lives." - **Mutiat Musa (Therapist, Baltimore, Maryland, United States of America)**

"The key word for this book is empathy. Eseosa will teach you how to truly cultivate empathy in your heart. It is a must-read for people who care for vulnerable individuals. Even health care professionals and social workers of experience can benefit from this precious perspective on their client's hurt." - **Sara-Kyanna Obas (Registered Clinician Nurse, Montreal, Quebec, Canada)**

"Anyone that reads Healing Growing Hearts by Eseosa Omoregie will immediately be struck by the candid way the author examines the issues surrounding children affected by many conditions and circumstances. The author's professional experience as a social worker and her personal passion to care for children are clearly evident. In Chapter Five the author brings to light the issues and challenges of dealing with abuse when complicated by alcohol and drug abuse.

Omoregie uses individual case studies to illustrate and discuss specific issues and how treatment is impacted. As a 30-year law enforcement executive and higher education criminal justice professional, I found this book extremely useful in understanding the social and clinical dynamics related to children in crisis. I recommend other criminal justice professionals use this book to learn and teach in a variety of criminal justice classes." - **Prof. William Schievella (Law Enforcement Executive and Professor of Criminal Justice at Saint Elizabeth University, Morristown, NJ)**

"Healing Growing Hearts is a comprehensive, culturally aware, and deeply empathetic exploration of the many challenges faced by children and youth experiencing trauma, neglect, systemic barriers, and social inequities. Across its chapters, the book weaves together rigorous research, global and local cultural perspectives, and powerful case studies that humanize the statistics and give voice to lived experiences. Each chapter provides a thoughtful balance between context, emotional resonance, and practical strategies, making it relevant not only to social workers, educators, and mental health professionals but also to caregivers, policy advocates, and community leaders.

Chapter Five's examination of child neglect is a strong example of the book's ability to combine definitions, prevention strategies, and stories that show the nuanced causes and impacts of neglect. Chapter Six expands the conversation to at-risk children, offering culturally diverse prevention approaches while emphasizing protective factors. Chapter Seven's focus on vulnerable youth blends statistical analysis with personal narratives, while Chapter Eight highlights the transformative role of intentional, sustained support systems. Chapters Nine through Eleven address some of the most urgent and sensitive areas: children in need of care and protection, those in conflict with the law, and those exposed to armed conflict, presenting trauma-informed, culturally grounded, and community-centered approaches to healing.

Healing Growing Hearts is a timely and impactful resource that affirms the resilience of children and youth while offering actionable guidance for those committed to supporting them. Its integration of cultural perspectives, legal frameworks, and practical tools makes it not only informative but transformative, with the potential to influence both practice and policy." - **Alfred Achoba (Executive Director, Canadian Mental Health Association, Kamloops Branch)**

TABLE OF CONTENT

Copyright Page --- ii
Dedication -- iii
Acknowledgments --------------------------------------- iv
Disclosure Statement ------------------------------------ vi
Peer Reviews -- vii
Table Of Content --- x
Introduction --- xi

Chapter 1: ***Defining Key Concepts*** *(Page 1)*

Chapter 2: ***Healing From Sexual Abuse & Exploitation*** *(Page 25)*

Chapter 3: ***Healing Path For Grieving Children & Youth*** *(Page 48)*

Chapter 4: ***Healing For Children & Youth in Conflict With The Law*** *(Page 69)*

Chapter 5: ***Healing For Children & Youth With Alcohol Codependency*** *(Page 92)*

Chapter 6: ***Healing For Children & Youth With Estranged Parent/Guardian Relationships*** *(Page 110)*

Chapter 7: ***Healing For Children & Youth With Disabilities*** *(Page 132)*

Chapter 8: ***Healing For Children & Youth In Foster Care Systems*** *(Page 155)*

Chapter 9: ***Healing For Migrant And Displaced Children & Youth*** *(Page 172)*

Chapter 10: ***Healing For Families In Crime Or Military Zones*** *(Page 191)*

References *(Page 207)*

INTRODUCTION

When we think about children and youth, what often comes to mind is innocence, energy, and potential. We see the future reflected in their eyes, which are ever vibrant and full of possibilities.

However, for many young people, life is not as simple as it seems. Behind their smiles may lie stories of pain, trauma, and unimaginable challenges. As someone who has worked closely with children and youth across various settings, this book is borne out of my personal experiences. It is my way of pouring out lessons, reflections, and stories with the hope of making a difference in the lives of young people.

Healing Growing Hearts is not just another book to pick up from a shelf. It is not a lengthy academic text filled with theories that feel far removed from real life. Instead, this book is deeply personal, practical, and intentional. It was written for those who have dedicated themselves to walking alongside young people—parents, caregivers, teachers, social workers, health professionals, mentors, survivors, and anyone with a heart for children. It is also written for those who have themselves lived through pain and now find themselves raising or supporting the next generation.

This book draws from real-life situations and stories, not to sensationalize trauma, but to show that healing is possible. It spans across different cultural and societal backgrounds, because trauma and healing are not limited to one place or people. Whether in Canada or elsewhere in the world, children and youth today are facing increasingly complex issues from abuse, addiction, loss, extending to systemic barriers and identity struggles.

As society evolves, our methods of care and support must evolve accordingly. With rapid technological growth, shifting cultural values, and increased exposure to global crises, our young people are carrying emotional burdens that demand more thoughtful and flexible responses. For this reason, we as caregivers, professionals, and community members can no longer rely solely on outdated models or one-size-fits-all strategies. We must be willing to adapt, to learn, and to approach each child and youth with both wisdom and empathy.

The heart of this book is healing. It explores what it means to walk with children and youth through their pain, not necessarily to fix them, but to help them find the strength within themselves to move forward. Each chapter focuses on different experiences, from sexual abuse and exploitation to grief, legal conflict, addiction in the home, displacement, and disabilities. You can agree with me that these are all lived realities for many children around the world. Some chapters also highlight complex family dynamics such as parenting through addiction, parental incarceration, and estrangement *(plus the impact these situations have on a young person's emotional development)*.

While the chapters are structured around specific themes, the approaches used throughout the book remain consistent. A trauma-informed lens is essential, as it helps us see behavior through the eyes of pain and survival. Cultural sensitivity is another cornerstone, as healing must always consider the values, identity, and traditions of those involved. Storytelling is used as a bridge to connect, to normalize, and to inspire. Finally, a strength-based approach is woven throughout, reminding us that children are not defined by what they've been through, but by who they can become.

This book is not meant to be read in one sitting. Some sections may be heavy or triggering, and that's okay. Readers are encouraged to pause when needed, to take care of themselves, and to process at their own pace. Healing is a journey, not a race.

At the end of every chapter, I offer reflections for those who support others—survivors, parents, foster carers, professionals, and care workers. Their healing matters too. To care for others, we must also care for ourselves. This book ends not with a solution, but with an invitation to keep learning, growing, and healing together.

Healing Growing Hearts is more than a collection of ideas. It is a companion for anyone walking with young people through pain and into purpose. My hope is that through these words, you will find not just understanding, but also renewed courage to support the children and youth in your life with greater compassion, creativity, and care.

CHAPTER ONE
DEFINING KEY CONCEPTS

We live in a world of countless societal tags. If you walk into any social services office, flip through any case file, or sit in on any team meeting about vulnerable young people, you'll read or hear terms like at-risk, traumatized, neglected, disadvantaged, and others. These words roll off our tongues so easily, don't they? We use them in reports, check them off on forms, and slot them into neat categories that help us in the work we do.

But here's what I want you to remember as we journey through the pages of this book.

Behind every single one of these labels is a human being. A child with a mixture of hopes and fears. A teenager trying to figure out who they are in a world that hasn't felt safe to them. A young person whose story is heartbreaking yet beautiful, such that no storyline could ever capture.

When we say a child or youth has been sexually abused or exploited, we are not just talking about a category of harm. We are talking about a young person whose sense of safety, trust, and bodily autonomy have been tampered with. When we describe someone as grieving, we're not simply noting a stage in a process. We are (essentially) acknowledging an individual whose world has been turned upside down by loss, who might be angry at God, at life, at everyone who still has what they have lost.

Think about that child or youth who has endured maltreatment and malnutrition without the hope of a better situation. When we write "foster care placement" in their file, are we capturing what it feels like to

We live in a world of countless societal tags. If you walk into any social services office, flip through any case file, or sit in on any team meeting about vulnerable young people, you'll read or hear terms like at-risk, traumatized, neglected, disadvantaged, and others. These words roll off our tongues so easily, don't they? We use them in reports, check them off on forms, and slot them into neat categories that help us in the work we do.

But here's what I want you to remember as we journey through the pages of this book.

Behind every single one of these labels is a human being. A child with a mixture of hopes and fears. A teenager trying to figure out who they are in a world that hasn't felt safe to them. A young person whose story is heartbreaking yet beautiful, such that no storyline could ever capture.

When we say a child or youth has been sexually abused or exploited, we are not just talking about a category of harm. We are talking about a young person whose sense of safety, trust, and bodily autonomy have been tampered with. When we describe someone as grieving, we're not simply noting a stage in a process. We are (essentially) acknowledging an individual whose world has been turned upside down by loss, who might be angry at God, at life, at everyone who still has what they have lost.

Think about that child or youth who has endured maltreatment and malnutrition without the hope of a better situation. When we write "foster care placement" in their file, are we capturing what it feels like to never quite belong anywhere? To always be the outsider looking in at families who seem to have figured out what they are still searching for?

Consider the young boy or girl who turns to substances. They may not intrinsically be difficult, but acting out the script of one under substance abuse tends to be the only way they have learned to quiet the voices in their head. To them, substance abuse may not seem like a behaviour that should be corrected, but a coping mechanism borne from pain that runs deeper than most of us can imagine.

These conditions (and more) are situations that many children and youths face, every single day. They are the invisible wounds that affect how they see themselves, how they relate with others, and how they move through a world that often feels unpredictable and unsafe, and in this chapter, we are getting to the heart of what these words really mean.

And here is why this matters so much to me. When we truly understand what we are dealing with, when we see beyond the societal tags to the real human experiences beneath them, everything changes. Our responses should become more thoughtful, our interventions should become more effective, and our compassion should become more genuine. We will begin to address root causes, rather than treat symptoms, and go beyond managing behaviors to effect holistic healing.

In the pages that follow, we are going to take our time with these concepts. I am writing this book to a diverse audience, so I do not want to assume that every reader is on the same page. We are going to sit with every necessary definition and really examine what they mean in the lives of the young people we serve.
This is because a better understanding leads to better care, and is indeed, the first step in their healing journey.

We are not just going to define these experiences. We are going to help you recognize them when they walk into your life. We are going to give you the tools to respond with wisdom rather than just good intentions. We are also going to prepare you for the sacred work of walking alongside young people as they navigate some of life's most difficult terrain.

As social workers, healthcare professionals, parents, caregivers, teachers and religious leaders, the work ahead of us isn't easy. Some of what you'll read in the coming chapters will be difficult to process. You'll encounter realities that will break your heart and challenge everything you thought you knew about child protection and care for youths. But on the flipside, you will also discover the incredible capacity of young people to heal, to grow, to overcome even the most devastating circumstances when they have caring adults who truly understand their journey.

Get ready with me, as we give meaning to relevant terms that will aid a better understanding of subsequent chapters in this book. Let's go!

Children

By nature's design, every living being must pass through a stage of infancy. You were once a child, and so was I. The childhood stage is one that is often characterised by dependency, innocence, and vulnerability. Above all, children are known to be deeply impressionable, and that explains why notable experiences in a child's life could stick in their minds for a lifetime.

But who really is a child?

According to the United Nations Convention on the Rights of the Child (UNCRC), a child is anyone under the age of 18 (which is the legal age in many nations). These early years have the potential to create psychological and emotional templates that often play out in adulthood. It is important that we have this foundational knowledge, as it will make sense in other definitions we are yet to explore.

Children rely heavily on the adults around them to interpret life. For most children, their primary method of asking questions is through their actions and non-verbal cues, more than their voice. This means that a child may not be able to speak in the language that their parents or caregivers can understand, and even if they find language to what's happening within and around them, they may be unable to communicate such feelings, thoughts, and emotions due to inhibiting factors like fear and/or shame.

This is why abuse (which we will later consider) at this stage is so devastating, as it could distort a child's original configuration, and mar them for life if they do not heal.

In working with children, parents, caregivers and social workers must master the art of listening beyond words, observing without judgment, and asking the right questions. The child who speaks too little, and the one who talks too much could be hiding a story. Like I mentioned earlier, children often lack the language to say what's hurting them, so they tend to show us instead. And unless we know what to look for, we might miss the signs, and this could slow down their healing process.

Youth

The term "youth" generally refers to individuals between the ages of 15 and 29 years old. However, age alone doesn't capture the complexity of this stage. Youth is a season marked by the search for identity, independence, belonging, and purpose. It's a time when the influence of peers rises sharply, and the pull to explore personal freedom becomes stronger than ever. The problem is, many youths begin this journey without enough guidance, and in environments that may not be safe.

One thing I've come to realise in my years of working with youths is that the pressures they face today are far more layered than we often acknowledge. There's the internal pressure of trying to answer the question of identity, and then there is external pressure, expectations from family, school, religious bodies, and society at large. These expectations can feel like a weight around their necks, especially when paired with personal trauma, neglect, or abuse.

At this stage, many young people are caught between wanting to be seen as capable adults and still needing the safety and structure of childhood. They crave autonomy but may not yet have the emotional tools to make safe, wise decisions. That's why youth are particularly vulnerable to exploitation, often emotionally, sexually, psychologically, and financially. Their desire to be loved, accepted, and respected can be weaponized against them by those who know just how to manipulate those needs.

Sometimes, this vulnerability shows up in ways that are easy to misjudge. A teenager acting out in school might be silently grieving a traumatic experience. A withdrawn or rebellious youth might simply be protecting themselves from a world that hasn't been kind. The truth is, pain at this stage often disguises itself, and unless we approach youth with strategic inquisitiveness, compassion, and patience, we may end up punishing them for their wounds instead of helping them heal.

If we must get to the point of understanding youths better, we must speak in the language they understand. Getting the most from individuals in this age bracket requires tact, empathy, patience, humility, and a heart that truly cares and is willing to help. We must be willing to accept them in whatever state they find themselves, and professionally lead them through the process of healing.

Abuse

When you hear the word "abuse", what comes to your mind?

Defined in the simplest terms, abuse refers to any action or inaction that causes harm, injury, distress, or suffering to another person. It can be physical, emotional, psychological, sexual, verbal, spiritual, or even economic in nature.

According to the World Health Organization (WHO, 2002), abuse, especially in the context of children and vulnerable persons, includes "all forms of physical and/or emotional ill-treatment, sexual abuse, neglect or negligent treatment, and exploitation resulting in actual or potential harm." It is important to note the phrase "actual or potential", because the damage is not always immediate or obvious.

What makes abuse particularly complex is that it is often committed by people in positions of trust (parents, caregivers, relatives, teachers, religious figures, employers, or even peers). In these situations, the abused person may struggle to name the experience for what it truly is, either because they have been conditioned to normalize the behavior, or because they fear the consequences of speaking out.

This emotional confusion is one of the most crippling effects of abuse, and sadly, it is what allows it to continue.

Sex

Sex is one of the most misunderstood, misrepresented, and misused concepts in the world. Depending on one's upbringing, environment, culture, or personal experience, the word "sex" can provoke curiosity, fear, shame, confusion, or even trauma. Healthy and consensual sex in the right confines should not elicit any of those feelings, so if any or many of the aforelisted feelings are present, what happened was not sex.

What then is this much-talked-about sex?

Simply put, sex is that consensual physical and emotional act between individuals that is often an expression of intimacy, connection, and mutual desire. Biologically, sex refers to the reproductive function between sexes or genders. In the relational context, sex carries an emotional and psychological meaning which is built on trust, communication, and free will.

The World Health Organization (2006) describes sexual health as "a state of physical, emotional, mental, and social well-being in relation to sexuality." Within this framework, sex is meant to be respectful, safe, pleasurable, and free from coercion or violence.

However, this definition doesn't reflect the lived reality of many, particularly those who have been victims of sexual violence. And this is where the lines begin to blur, not because they should, but because abusers intentionally blur them. For this reason, it is important to note that rape is not sex. Manipulation is not sex. Threats are not sex. Coercion, guilt-tripping, blackmail, and fear are not sex. These are acts of control and aggression, and they must never be mistaken for intimacy.

True sex cannot exist without consent, and consent must be given freely, enthusiastically, and without pressure of any kind. This means that any form of sexual activity involving a child, youth, or anyone who is unable to give full and informed consent is not sex. The same applies when the act is forced, tricked, or manipulated. No matter what the abuser says, what the victim wore, or how long the relationship had lasted, without formal consent, it is not sex, but violence.

As professionals, caregivers, educators, or even survivors reading this, we must begin to redefine sex in ways that are healing, honest, and trauma-informed. We must lead the next generation to a place of understanding that sex is not a transaction, a reward, or a tool for approval, and that no one has the right to access or explore another person's body against their will.

The conversation around sex must become safer, clearer, and more truthful. Silence breeds confusion, and confusion allows abuse to flourish. When we intentionally educate properly about what sex truly is, and what it is not, we will empower individuals to make healthy and informed choices. We will also protect them from being abused, exploited, and manipulated.

Sexual Abuse

Having clarified what sex is and what it is not, I will like that we quickly follow up with another crucial subject connected to sex, which is sexual abuse. This is important because sexual abuse is far more common than most people, survivors especially, are willing to admit.

Sexual abuse, just like sex, is one of those topics that makes most people uncomfortable. We would rather not think about it, talk about it, or acknowledge how common its occurence could actually be. Sexual abuse happens everywhere across the globe, and no geography, religion, race, or social status is immune to its effects.
It is interesting to know that when most people think of sexual abuse, what comes to their mind is rape, and other violent forms of sexual predation by unfamiliar figures. While these ugly situations play out for real, they represent only a small fraction of sexual abuse cases. The reality is much more complex and, in many ways, more disturbing.

Research shows that approximately 90% of children who experience sexual abuse know their perpetrator (Darkness to Light, 2015). These are often people the child trusts, including family members, family friends, teachers, coaches, religious leaders, or other authority figures. This cannot be an accident, but proves that sexual predators deliberately build relationships with these children and their families to gain access and trust.

Dr. Anna Salter, a renowned expert on sexual offenders, explains that perpetrators are often skilled at reading children and identifying those who are particularly vulnerable, that is, children who are lonely, seeking attention, or dealing with family problems (Salter, 2003). These predators often disguise as the present, providing, and understanding adult who listens and cares when no one else does. And for children and youths whose minds are impressionable, it could be difficult to differentiate what is real from what is not.

Let us now establish the fact that sexual abuse do not happen suddenly. There is such a term called grooming, which is the process by which perpetrators prepare children for abuse. It is usually well planned over a generous period, and executed at the point where the minds and bodies of their target comes fully under their control.

Grooming typically begins with trust-building. The perpetrator establishes themselves as helpful, understanding, and special in the life of their target. In the case of children, they might volunteer to babysit the child, offer to help with homework, or become the adult they turn to when they have problems. At the grooming stage, they usually pay attention to what their target needs or lacks, and providing these necessities is always often, a means to their selfish ends.

As time progresses, they subtly begin to introduce the child or youth to sexual content. They also begin to cross physical boundaries, often expressed in the way they touch sensitive body parts and make it look harmless, crack inappropriate jokes, expose them to sexual materials, and eventually normalize sexual conversations and contact, little by little.

Sexual Exploitation

While we can agree that sexual abuse and sexual exploitation are acts of sexual violation, we must understand the difference between the both of them, especially as parents and caregivers. According to ECPAT International, sexual exploitation of children is fundamentally "a crime involving a child in sexual activity in exchange for remuneration or any other form of consideration" (ECPAT International, 2020). In simpler terms, someone benefits from a young person's vulnerability, and that benefit drives the ongoing abuse.

Sexual exploitation involves manipulating, coercing, or deceiving someone into sexual activity in exchange for something. That something might be money, shelter, gifts, food, affection, safety, or even social approval. This is often done without the express (or informed) consent of the other party.

Research have proven that children and adolescents cannot make free and informed choices when survival needs, desperation, or emotional manipulation are at play (Victims of Trafficking and Violence Protection Act, 2000).

I have heard (and I am sure you have read) many sad stories where young folks are tricked into situations where they cannot help themselves, and when all doors seem closed, sex is presented as the way out. We have seen situations where celebrities are being bullied into paying huge amounts of money, just so that private pictures or videos of them won't be leaked. We see children and youths living in poverty being recruited into prostitution, or sexual performances in return for one material benefit or the other.

One of the major distinctions between sexual abuse and sexual exploitation lies in this transactional element. While abuse is often personal and secretive, exploitation has a layer of exchange where the abuser gets something tangible in return for the harm (often disguised as reward) they inflict. This might be money, labour, status, or simply the power that comes from controlling another person.

Dr. Rachel Lloyd, founder of GEMS (Girls Educational and Mentoring Services) and a survivor herself, explains that many young people enter exploitative situations through what appears to be a relationship (Lloyd, 2011). The exploiter doesn't present themselves as a predator. Instead, they position themselves as a boyfriend, a mentor, or someone who truly cares. They identify what the young person needs most and provide it, thereby (subtly) creating a sense of debt and obligation.

Sexual exploitation tends to be more systemic than individual sexual abuse. That's because it is not always one abuser operating alone; it can involve entire networks, both online and offline. We see this play out even in corporate settings where sex is the ultimate price to pay for employment, promotion, or high-profile positions. Academic institutions are not left out, as there is such a thing as Sex For Grades—a situation where a student is coerced into having sex with a lecturer or tutor, in exchange for academic grades.

In a nutshell, sexual abuse involves direct physical contact (touching, kissing, fondling, rubbing, oral sex, or penetration of the vagina or anus) while sexual exploitation is what I will describe as a dirty mind game.

Trauma

Dr. Judith Herman, one of the pioneering researchers in trauma studies, describes trauma as resulting from events that are "outside the range of usual human experience" and involve "intense fear, helplessness, loss of control, and threat of annihilation" (Herman, 2015).

Trauma usually appears in different forms. We have acute trauma, complex trauma, chronic abuse or neglect, and historical trauma that often gets passed down through generations. For young people, picture trauma as an instance where a teenager cannot concentrate in class because their mind and body is always scanning for threats to safety, or flares up in anger at the smallest frustration because their nervous system learned that aggression is the right response to such situations.

I would like us to understand that two individuals can experience the same event and have completely different trauma responses based on their age, support systems, previous experiences, and many other factors. Some children might develop Post-traumatic Stress Disorder (PTSD), while others might show signs of resilience on the outside, but struggle with anxiety, depression, or behavioural disorders.

The body keeps the score, as trauma researcher Dr. Bessel van der Kolk famously wrote (van der Kolk, 2014). Trauma lives in the body long after the mind tries to forget. This is why traditional talk therapy alone often isn't enough for trauma survivors. Their bodies need to learn safety again, to release the tension and hypervigilance that trauma creates.

The good news is that understanding trauma has changed how we care for children and young people. Trauma-informed care recognizes that challenging behaviors are often symptoms of underlying trauma, not necessarily character flaws or defiance. When we ask the right questions, we open the door to healing rather than punishment. Recovery is possible, but it requires patience, understanding, and approaches that address both the mind and body's response to traumatic experiences.

Consent

Simply put, consent means freely given agreement to something. For the loop of consent to be complete, it must be informed, voluntary, ongoing, and given by someone who has the mental ability and legal capacity to make that decision..

Legally speaking, minors (persons under the age of 18) cannot give consent to sexual activity with adults because it is believed that children do not have the same decision-making capacity as adults, and that age and mental imbalance make true consent impossible. This does not mean that young people do not have a voice in what happens to them. The key message here is that age-appropriate consent means involving children and teenagers in decisions that affect them, while respecting their developing mind frames and protecting them from harm.

The concept of informed consent is especially important in healthcare and therapeutic settings. This means that young people (and their guardians) have the right to understand what is being proposed, what the risks and benefits are, and what alternatives are available before they agree to treatment. For adolescents and young adults, balancing self-will and protection can be challenging, particularly around sensitive issues like mental health treatment or reproductive health.

Be that as it may, I think it is high time that consent education is given its priority. Young people need to understand their rights and boundaries from an early age, and this is not limited to sexual consent, though that's important on its own.

Children should be taught that they have the right to say no to unwanted physical contact, that their feelings and preferences matter, and that they should respect other people's boundaries too.

Sexual & Gender-Based Violence

Sexual and Gender-Based Violence (often abbreviated as SGBV) refers to harmful acts that are committed against someone's will, and are based on socially constructed differences between males and females. According to the United Nations, SGBV includes "any act that inflicts physical, sexual or psychological harm or suffering on the basis of gender" (UN Women, 2021).

SGBV can take the form of sexual violence like rape, sexual assault, and sexual harassment. It also involves physical violence such as domestic abuse, harmful traditional practices, psychological and emotional violence, threats, intimidation, and other forceful behaviors. For children and young people, SGBV might also include infant marriage, female genital mutilation, and commercial sexual exploitation.

It is important to note that SGBV is largely perpetrated on people because of their gender, and those who carry out these acts often prey on the perceived weakness or naivety of their target, as a way to maintain dominance and control. For example, a man hitting a lady with the (wrong) mindset that she is female, and is therefore weak and would not be able to defend herself.

This also occurs within relationships where the targets thought they were safe. Research has shown that family members, intimate partners, and even authority figures sometimes use their power to harm or sexually abuse persons connected to them, rather than protect them.

Neglect

We can describe neglect as the not-so-obvious absence of care, attention, and provision that children need to survive. The Child

Welfare Information Gateway defines neglect as "the failure of a parent, guardian, or other caregiver to provide for a child's basic needs" (Child Welfare Information Gateway, 2019).

Physical neglect is what we often (and easily) observe. Talk about the child who does not have adequate food, clothing, shelter, or medical care, or the one who goes to school hungry every day, wearing the same dirty clothes, or has untreated medical conditions because no one cared enough to take them to see a doctor.

But then, neglect goes far beyond just physical needs. We have educational neglect, which occurs when children are not enrolled in school or do not have their basic or special educational needs met. We also have emotional neglect, which happens when children's emotional needs for love, attention, and support are often ignored. Medical neglect, which is one of the major forms of neglect, occurs when children don't receive necessary medical attention, as and when due.

There are other forms of neglect outside the aforementioned, but I won't go into details here. However, it is important to know that the effects of neglect can be as bad as that of abuse. Emotional neglect, for instance, could be the reason for a child or youth's delay in cognitive and social development.
It could also be the reason why they face challenges in the aspect of academics and relationships. Dr. Jonice Webb's research on emotional neglect shows that children who experience this form of neglect often struggle with feelings of emptiness, difficulty identifying emotions, and challenges in relationships throughout their lives (Webb, 2012).

Grief & Loss

When I talk about grief, I am talking about the emotional, physical, and psychological response we have when we lose something or someone we value. Loss, on the other hand, is the actual event that brings about grief. The American Psychological Association describes grief as a "multifaceted response to loss, particularly the loss of someone or something with which a bond was formed" (APA, 2023). Notice the word multifaceted.

What really amazes me is how differently kids handle grief compared to adults. According to The National Child Traumatic Stress Network, young people often experience grief in "pockets," dipping into sorrow and popping back out to play (NCTSN, 2019). The knowledge of this is particularly important to social workers, health professionals, parents and caregivers, as it will inform their choice of approach to healing.

There are five stages of grief as introduced by Kübler-Ross and later refined with David Kessler (Kübler-Ross & Kessler, 2005). These stages are: denial, anger, bargaining, depression, and acceptance. Knowing these stages is helpful, but in reality, this sequence may differ from person to person. That means, it is possible for anger to be the first emotion you feel when grief hits you, before you even begin to act in denial, or progress through other stages.

Developmental factors significantly influence how young people experience and express grief. Young children might not fully understand the permanence of death and may repeatedly ask when the deceased person is coming back.

Teenagers might struggle with grief because it forces them to confront their own mortality, and the unpredictability of life just when they're trying to establish independence and identity. Some young people throw themselves into activities to avoid the pain, while others might withdraw completely.

Addiction/Dependency

When we see a young person struggling with substance use or abuse, our first instinct is to focus on the substances themselves (alcohol, hard drugs and pills). However, addiction and dependency do not begin with substances in the picture. Beneath the substances lie pain, trauma, disconnection, and the desperate human need to feel different and better. Dr. Gabor Maté, a renowned expert on addiction, argues that addiction is not a choice or a disease, but an adaptation to trauma and emotional pain (Maté, 2008).

For young people, the path to addiction often begins with what Dr. Maté calls "adverse childhood experiences" This could be trauma, abuse, neglect, or other early life stressors that leave them struggling to regulate their emotions and cope with life's challenges. Substances become a form of self-medication, a way to numb emotional pain, quiet anxiety, escape from trauma memories, or simply feel normal in a world that often feels overwhelming and unsafe.

It is important to me that we understand the difference between substance use, abuse, and dependency. Many teenagers experiment with substances as part of normal adolescent risk-taking and identity exploration. Substance abuse occurs when use begins to interfere with important life activities like school, relationships, or health. Dependency involves both physical and psychological reliance on substances, where stopping use leads to withdrawal symptoms and where increasing amounts are needed to achieve the same effect.

The adolescent brain is particularly vulnerable to addiction because it is still developing, especially the prefrontal cortex that is responsible for decision-making, impulse control, and understanding consequences. This means that young people who use substances face higher risks of developing addiction than adults who begin using the same substances later in life. The earlier someone begins using substances, the greater their risk of developing a substance use disorder (SAMHSA, 2020).

Mental Health

I would like us to view mental health, not just as the absence of mental illness, but as a state of emotional, psychological, and social well-being that affects how people (children and youths in this context) think, feel, and act.

A person's state of mental health influences how they handle stress, relate with people, and make choices. Good mental health is particularly necessary for children and youths to develop effectively, build and maintain healthy relationships, achieve their goals in academics, and otherwise.

For children and youth, mental health is closely connected to their developmental stage. What is normal and healthy to a six-year-old child, may look different to a sixteen-year-old youth. Young children are still learning to identify and express their emotions, while teenagers are in the process of identity formation, increased independence, and complex social relationships.

Mental health conditions in young people can include anxiety disorders, depression, Attention-Deficit/Hyperactivity Disorder (ADHD), eating disorders, bipolar disorder, and emerging personality disorders. According to the National Institute of Mental Health, nearly 32% of adolescents experience an anxiety disorder, and about 13% experience a major depressive episode (NIMH, 2021).

Disability

We need to make peace with the fact that disability does not intrinsically mean the absence of ability in an individual, but is a part of human diversity. So, just as we have friends who are Black, White, Caucasian or Hispanic, we also have friends who, for some reason, may not be able to see, hear, walk, or effectively use certain organs in their bodies.

The World Health Organization defines disability as resulting from "the interaction between individuals with a health condition and barriers in their environment" (WHO, 2021). This social construct of disability makes us see beyond what is wrong with a person, to what is wrong with environments that exclude or discriminate against people living with disabilities.

Children and youth with disabilities often face unique challenges that go far beyond their specific impairments. They may encounter physical barriers like inaccessible buildings or transportation, communication barriers when information isn't provided in ways they can understand, or attitudinal barriers when others hold low expectations or prejudiced views about their capabilities. These barriers, not their disabilities themselves, are often what create the most significant challenges in their lives.

Physical disabilities might affect mobility (how they move), coordination, or strength. Intellectual disabilities impact learning, problem-solving, and adaptive functioning. Sensory disabilities affect vision or hearing. Mental health conditions can also be considered disabilities when they limit major life activities to a large extent.

From my experience, most people hold the view that persons living with disabilities always have a poor quality of life or are bound to suffer, but from research, children and adults with disabilities report life satisfaction levels similar to those without disabilities when they have appropriate support and access to opportunities (Albrecht & Devlieger, 1999).

Stigma

A renowned Sociologist, Erving Goffman described stigma as a "deeply discrediting" attribute that reduces someone "from a whole and usual person to a tainted, discounted one" (Goffman, 1963). Stigma could be worse for children and young people, because it greatly affects their developing sense of self and belonging. Simply put, stigma is a negative attitude or belief that leads to discrimination, exclusion, or unfair treatment of someone based on a particular characteristic or condition (WHO, 2017).

There are different types of stigma we should be aware of. The first and most common is public stigma, which refers to the negative attitudes and discriminatory behaviours that society holds toward stigmatized individuals or groups. Second to this is structural stigma, a situation where policies and practices by institutions limit opportunities for stigmatized individuals.

The most disturbing form of stigma, in my opinion, is self-stigma. This happens when people internalize negative stereotypes about themselves and begin to see themselves as less worthy or capable because of their condition or (often negative) experiences.

Common reasons children and youth face stigma include but are not limited to: negative mental health conditions, physical disabilities, family circumstances like poverty or incarceration, health status, immigration status, or experiences like abuse or trauma. For example, a young person living with HIV, and whose case was not properly managed, might face public stigma from peers who see them as bad examples, or people on death row, which may not be true.

Stigma, if not addressed, can lead to isolation, low self-esteem, increased mental health problems, and avoidance of seeking help when needed. It can also affect educational achievement negatively, limit future opportunities, and strain family relationships. For many young people, the stigma attached to their condition or experience has been more damaging than the condition itself, and this could interfere with their healing process.

Estranged Relationships

When discussing estranged relationships in the context of vulnerable children and youths, we are usually referring to serious break-offs in family relationships, often between children and their parents or caregivers.

Estrangement involves a significant (and often lasting) disconnection that leaves young people without the family support that most of us take for granted.

This can happen as a result of abuse or neglect, where young people have to distance themselves from family members for their own safety and well-being. It could also happen as a result of conflicts over values, faith, cultural or religious differences, or life choices that should be personal.

Foster Care

The foster care system was designed to be a temporary safe haven for children who can't live with their biological families due to abuse, neglect, or other serious family problems. The main objective of the foster care system is to provide these children with stable, nurturing care while working toward either reunifying them with their families or matching them with permanent adoptive homes.

Children enrolled on the foster care system have already experienced significant trauma and loss. They have been migrated from the known to the unknown, and even when such migration or removal was necessary for their safety, it represents another phase of loss in young lives that have often already experienced significant loss.

Dr. Bruce Perry's research shows that children in foster care have typically experienced multiple traumatic events before even entering the system (Perry, 2006). The foster care system itself can be traumatizing (as many children undergo multiple placements without finding stability); however, foster care can also be transformative when handled effectively.

Migration/Displacement

When we talk about young people who've been forced to leave their homes, we are talking about some of the most resilient (and vulnerable) individuals you will ever meet.

Migration and displacement can happen as a result of fleeing war zones, sites of natural disasters, and even unsupportive environments. When this happens, these young people are put in a position where they have to rebuild their lives from scratch, and doing this often comes with invisible wounds from past experiences.

It is a different thing to move to somewhere new on your own, and a different thing to be forced out of your home with little or no warning. Voluntary migration can be tough on its own, but forced displacement is placing trauma upon trauma.

The journey itself often becomes another layer of trauma. Talk about dangerous border crossings, exploitation by smugglers, separation from family members, or months in overcrowded and poorly managed refugee camps. These experiences have a high-level psychological impact on children and youth, and they show up in many ways.

Human Trafficking

Human trafficking happens when people (often powerful or influential people) use force, lies, or manipulation to make someone else work or perform sexual acts for money against their will. And it is even more horrifying when it involves kids and teenagers. To be clear, any time a minor is involved in commercial sex, that is a case of trafficking, period. There's no such thing as a willing child participant because children do not have the capability to consent to being sold for sex.

The words we use when discussing issues like this matter a lot, and we must be careful while using them. For example, it is not right to say "child prostitutes" or "teen sex workers". These terms make it sound like the children or youth involved made an informed decision to do what they found themselves doing. They are simply victims of commercial sexual exploitation, crime victims who need help, and not criminals who deserve punishment.

We must understand that traffickers have mastered the art of spotting vulnerable young people and their most pressing needs, and they swoop in to offer exactly what these young people are missing.

When they do this, the victims of this act develop trauma bonds with their traffickers, which make them feel loyal and protective towards the very people destroying their lives. This explains why it is sometimes difficult to rescue and bring victims of trafficking to a point of total healing.

Violence

Violence is simply the use of force or power to hurt someone else, yourself, or a group of people. It includes threatening someone, causing emotional pain, or creating systems that prevent people from getting what they need, which is important to them. When we have an understanding of what violence could mean to us as grown-ups, we will better understand how much it could negatively impact the lives of children and youths, directly and indirectly.

Irrespective of the nature or cause of violence, one thing we all can agree on is that violence does not leave anyone the same way it met them.

Victims of communal clashes will never have things the same way they were before such an occurrence. Families who have lived to experience a war of any sort will never forget such an experience, and children living with parents who practice domestic violence will, if not helped, begin to think it is normal.

Young people exposed to ongoing violence may develop Post-traumatic Stress Disorder (PTSD), depression, or turn to substances to cope. They might struggle with aggression, find it nearly impossible to trust others, or completely withdraw from relationships that could help them heal.

Caregiver

A caregiver is someone who provides care, support, and assistance to another person who needs help with daily activities, health management, or general well-being. Caregivers can be family members, friends, volunteers, or professionals, and their work spans across all ages and conditions of those they serve.

The scope of caregiving is typically broad and can range from helping an aging parent with grocery shopping and medication management to providing round-the-clock care for a child with special needs, or supporting a spouse through their treatment process.

Some caregivers assist with basic activities of daily living like bathing, dressing, and eating, while others provide emotional support, coordinate medical appointments, manage finances, or simply offer companionship to combat loneliness and isolation.

Caregivers can also stand in as parents in events where the attention or presence of a young person's parent figure is needed.

Healing

Healing is a profound and deeply personal process that encompasses much more than the simple absence of symptoms or the mending of physical wounds. It represents a journey toward wholeness, integration, and renewed vitality that can occur on physical, emotional, mental, and spiritual levels. Medical treatments can cure diseases or repair injuries, but healing involves the broader restoration of a person's sense of well-being, purpose, and connection to themselves and others.

Unlike the medical model that often focuses on identifying problems and applying specific treatments, healing acknowledges that each person's path toward wellness is unique and influenced by countless factors, including their history, relationships, beliefs, cultural background, and personal resources. What promotes healing for one person may not work for another, and what helps someone at one stage of their journey may be different from what they need later on.

Lest I forget, I have to mention that healing is not just about returning to a previous state or pretending that difficult experiences never happened. Instead, it's about finding ways to integrate all of our experiences, both the joyful and the painful, into a beautiful sense of self that allows us to move forward with greater wisdom, resilience, and compassion. This perspective recognizes that sometimes our greatest growth and strength come from working through our most challenging experiences.

Survivor

As you read through the subsequent chapters in this book, you will find the term survivor being used multiple times. It is therefore important that we establish the meaning of what we mean by a survivor, early on.

The word survivor represents someone who has lived through and continues to navigate the aftermath of traumatic, dangerous, or life-threatening experiences. Since it is a more empowering word, we have chosen to use that instead of words like "victim" or "casualty".

Survivors come from all walks of life, and have endured many different types of experiences. Some are survivors of violence, abuse, or assault.

Others have survived accidents, natural disasters, serious illnesses, or life-threatening situations. There are survivors of war, genocide, persecution, or oppression. Some have survived addiction, mental health crises, or suicide attempts.

What is common among all survivors is not the specific nature of their experiences, but their act of persisting through circumstances that threatened their physical, emotional, or psychological well-being.

Support System

A support system is the network of people, resources, and relationships that provide emotional, practical, and sometimes financial assistance to help someone go through life's challenges and maintain their well-being.

Look at it like a safe space made up of people who can catch you when you fall, celebrate your successes, provide guidance when you're unsure of your direction, and help you get out of an unpleasant situation. These systems can be formal or informal, large or small, and they often evolve and change throughout different phases of our lives.

The strength and effectiveness of a support system isn't necessarily measured by its size, but by the quality of connections and how well it meets a person's needs. Some people do well with large, diverse networks, while others prefer smaller or close circles of support. What matters most is that the relationships are characterized by trust, reciprocity, and genuine care.

A healthy support system should enhance rather than drain a person's energy, provide both emotional and practical assistance when needed, and respect boundaries and individual choices.

***

Having examined these key concepts at their most basic levels, I am certain that the use of all these terms in subsequent chapters will be well understood in the context of their use. Keep these definitions at heart, as we will make reference to them while we progress.

CHAPTER TWO
HEALING FROM SEXUAL ABUSE & EXPLOITATION

"Everyone shall be free from sexuality related violence and coercion, including rape, sexual abuse, sexual harassment, bullying, sexual exploitation and slavery, trafficking for purposes of sexual exploitation, virginity testing, and violence committed because of real or perceived sexual practices." - UN Declaration of Sexual Rights.

In all my years as a social worker, I have met pain dressed in many different clothes, but nothing prepared me for the day I met this young lady. Let's call her

From my initial assessment, Anita was in her prime years, seated at one end of the client's room. She didn't speak much that day, barely looked at anyone, and when she did, her gaze felt like it had traveled through too much darkness to still believe in light.

What I would later learn about Anita's story, from the grooming, drug dependency, the nights she couldn't remember, and the ones she could never forget, would change the way I approached this work forever. On that first day, all I could do was offer her a listening ear, a reassuring smile, and wide arms while I sat quietly on the other end of the couch, present and immersed in the moment.

Anita's case wasn't isolated. Far from it. According to a recent global study by the World Health Organization, approximately 1 in 5 women and 1 in 13 men report being sexually abused as children. You see, reports like this usually do not sound as scary as they should be, until a loved one, a sibling, a ward under our care, a coworker, neighbor, or even us, falls victim to sexual abuse.

More disturbing is the fact that for every case reported, many more remain buried under fear, shame, or disbelief. And here lies the bigger problem.

> *"Young people who have endured sexual abuse or exploitation often do not express their feelings in obvious or traditional ways. Instead, their emotional distress may emerge through changes in behavior—such as shifts in how they relate with caregivers, peers, family, or authority figures. It may also be reflected in high-risk behaviors like substance misuse, legal troubles, or unsafe sexual activity."* - Eseosa Omoregie

From my experience working with persons in this category, I have observed that sexual abuse and exploitation usually do not end with the bruises sustained or trauma experienced. It almost always shows up as anxiety, anger, silence, or recklessness.

Sometimes, these emotions are buried so deeply that even the survivor doubts if what happened really happened. At other times, too often, these traumas are recycled across generations, and woven into the silences families keep, the cultural norms that excuse abuse, or the systems that fail to protect the most vulnerable.

Maybe that is you. Maybe you picked this book because you've been there, or maybe you're a caregiver, a friend, or a frontline worker trying to understand how to walk this road with someone you love or serve. Whatever the reason, you belong here.

And trust me when I say that this book in your hand is a safe space for everyone who has been through this journey. My experience in this field has taught me that healing could be found in the most unlikely of places and situations. It could be a few kind words, a supportive disposition, and attentive ears that listen without judgment and condescension. Sometimes, it could also be found in books like this, where someone finally finds language for their pain, or realizes for the first time that what happened to them was not their making.

In this chapter, we will examine some cases related to sexual abuse and exploitation, and explore the various models and approaches to healing.

First-Hand Work With Survivors

a) Western Residential Setting

(Anita's story continued)

Upon my first meeting with Anita, she had a history of sexual abuse dating back to childhood, struggles with substance dependency, and a family system marked by violence and intergenerational trauma rooted in her Indigenous heritage. Like many of the young women I worked with, Anita's story wasn't just about one traumatic event but rather a collection of experiences that had shaped her understanding of herself and her place in the world.

Beyond her trauma history, Anita was an embodiment of strength, if you ask me. She had been placed in our care after a series of incidents that highlighted her vulnerability to exploitation. The circumstances that brought her to us were painful: she had been found in situations where adults had taken advantage of her trauma responses and survival mechanisms. Her substance use, which had begun as a way to numb the pain of early abuse, had become another tool that predators used to manipulate and control her.

Anita's Western background carried with it the weight of historical trauma, passed down through generations. I know this because my probe led to the discovery that her family, while loving in their own way, struggled with their own untreated trauma. This created an environment where healthy attachment and safety were far from her. She had learned to survive by becoming hypervigilant, by reading the room before anyone else, and by making herself useful in ways that often put her at risk.

The gravity of Anita's situation became more apparent as I spent time with her and began to understand the full scope of what she had endured. The sexual abuse she experienced in childhood had occurred within her extended family network, perpetrated by someone she should have been able to trust. This early betrayal had fractured her ability to form healthy attachments and left her with a nervous system that was constantly on high alert. The exploitation that followed did not just happen, but was a direct consequence of predators recognizing and targeting the vulnerabilities created by her earlier trauma.

As it is with most survivors, the substance use that had initially been a coping mechanism had evolved into a dependency that further complicated her ability to stay safe. When she was using them, her decision-making became impaired, and she was more likely to end up in dangerous situations. The cycle was vicious: trauma led to substance use, which led to increased vulnerability, which led to more trauma. Her family relationships, already strained by their own trauma responses, became increasingly fractured as they struggled to understand and support her while managing their own pain.

One sad observation I had was seeing Anita internalize the messages that her trauma had taught her about her worth and value. She believed, on a deep level, that her primary value to others was sexual. You know, prolonged trauma has a way of making you think that you somehow deserve the treatment you receive.

This was the state of Anita before healing. These beliefs were not conscious thoughts, but rather deeply embedded assumptions that guided her behavior and choices.

Signs and Symptoms of Sexual Abuse & Exploitation
(in Anita's case)

Working with Anita, I observed numerous indicators that are commonly associated with sexual abuse and exploitation. Her sense of hypervigilance and alertness, even in a safe environment, was one of the most prominent signs. This state of chronic alertness is a hallmark of trauma exposure and reflects the nervous system's adaptation to perceived ongoing danger.

Anita also displayed significant dissociative symptoms, which research shows are common among survivors of childhood sexual abuse. During times of stress or when triggered by trauma reminders, she would appear to "zone out," becoming emotionally and sometimes physically unresponsive. These episodes, which could last minutes or hours, represented her mind's protective mechanism of disconnecting from overwhelming experiences (Herman, 2015). She often had difficulty remembering these periods, which is consistent with trauma-related memory disruption documented in clinical literature.

Anita's substance use patterns were consistent with research showing that individuals who experience childhood sexual abuse are significantly more likely to develop substance use disorders. For her, alcohol and drugs served multiple functions: they numbed emotional pain, helped her sleep, and paradoxically, sometimes made her feel more in control of her body and experiences. However, they also increased her vulnerability to further exploitation, as predators often target individuals whose judgment is impaired by substances.

Another way to know if one has been sexually abused or exploited (particularly helpful to social workers) is by getting sufficient information on their sexual behaviors and patterns. This could reveal where trauma is lurking, if expertly done. Survivors often alternate between periods of sexual avoidance and compulsive sexual behavior, both of which are recognized responses to sexual trauma. Sometimes, they would engage in risky sexual encounters as a way of trying to reclaim control over their sexuality, while at other times, they would shut down completely at any hint of physical intimacy.

One thing I have also discovered about young people who have experienced sexual abuse & exploitation is that some of them don't usually show outbursts of emotions through conventional ways. Instead, this could be shown through their negative attitudes towards their parents, caregivers, workers, friends, families, guardians, and even displaying high-risk behavior such as drug and alcohol dependency.

Anita's Healing Journey

Having understood that some traditional approaches can re-traumatize survivors in Western and Indigenous cultures, I committed to using a trauma-informed care framework from our very first interaction. This approach, developed through decades of research on trauma's impact on development and healing, recognizes that many behaviors labeled as "problematic" are adaptive responses to impossible situations (SAMHSA, 2014). Rather than asking *"What's wrong with you?"* trauma-informed care asks *"What happened to you?"* and *"How can we help you heal?"*

My first step in implementing trauma-informed care with Anita was establishing safety, both physical and emotional. I reassured her that she was in safe hands and did my best to ensure that there was transparency in our communication. Over time, trust was built, and that was one major step in her healing journey.

Central to trauma-informed care is the recognition that healing happens in relationship, and that the therapeutic relationship itself can be a vehicle for experiencing healthy attachment. With Anita, this meant moving at her pace, respecting her boundaries, and consistently demonstrating that I could be trusted with her story. I paid attention to small details that mattered to her, remembered things she told me, and showed up both as a professional and a friend.

One of the key discoveries in our work together was Anita's passion for makeup and photography. Traditional deficit-based approaches might have dismissed these interests as superficial or unrelated to her "real" problems. However, trauma-informed care emphasizes building on individual strengths and interests as pathways to healing.

I learned that makeup artistry gave Anita a sense of control over her appearance and identity, while photography allowed her to see beauty in the world around her and express her perspective in ways that words couldn't capture. Supporting these interests became a cornerstone of our work together, and thankfully, this strength-based approach did not just help her build her skills but also helped her develop a positive identity beyond her trauma history.

Trauma-informed care also emphasizes the importance of understanding how trauma impacts every aspect of a person's life, including their family and cultural context. Recognizing that Anita's Indigenous background was both a source of strength and a site of intergenerational trauma, I worked to connect her with Indigenous counselors and cultural supports. This culturally responsive approach acknowledged that healing needed to honor her identity and heritage rather than ignore or minimize it (Brave Heart, 2003).

The advocacy component of trauma-informed care was crucial in Anita's case. This meant serving as her voice in meetings with probation officers, healthcare providers, and other professionals who might not understand trauma's impact on behaviour and decision-making. I helped translate her trauma responses for providers and worked to ensure that all services she received were delivered through a trauma-informed lens.

Also, language and communication were fundamental aspects of our trauma-informed approach. Research shows that how we talk about trauma and its effects can either support healing or reinforce shame and self-blame (Knight, 2018). With Anita, this meant using person-first language, avoiding victim-blaming terminology, and consistently reinforcing that what happened to her was not her fault. When discussing her substance use, for example, I framed it as an understandable response to overwhelming pain rather than a moral failing or character defect.

The pacing of our work together was entirely determined by Anita's capacity and readiness, another key principle of trauma-informed care. Some days she was ready to engage deeply in difficult conversations, while other days she needed to focus on basic stabilization and safety. This flexible, responsive approach honored her autonomy and avoided the re-traumatization that can occur when survivors feel pressured to heal according to external timelines.

When Anita experienced difficulties or made choices that put her at risk, we approached these moments as opportunities to understand her triggers and develop better coping strategies rather than as evidence that she wasn't "trying hard enough." This non-judgmental approach was the way to go for someone who had internalized deep shame about her responses to trauma.

The collaborative nature of trauma-informed care meant that Anita was always the expert on her own experience, and my role was to provide support, resources, and professional expertise while honoring her person and self-determination. Together, we developed safety plans, identified triggers and coping strategies, and worked toward goals that she had defined for herself. This approach helped restore her sense of personal power and choice, which trauma had stolen from her.

The transformation I witnessed in Anita over the months we worked together was profound. She began to develop a sense of her worth that wasn't tied to other people's approval or sexual attention. Her substance use decreased as she developed healthier coping strategies and began to believe that she deserved care and protection. Most importantly, she started to envision a future for herself that included her passions and goals rather than just survival. The trauma-informed approach didn't erase her past, but it helped her integrate her experiences in a way that allowed her to move forward with strength, wisdom, and hope.

b) African Community Setting

(Kate's Story, as reported by a social worker in Nigeria)

"It takes a village to raise a child," goes the ancient African proverb, yet sometimes that same village must come together to heal one. In Nigeria, where one in four girls experiences sexual violence before age 18, according to UNICEF data, the power of community support becomes not just culturally significant but critically necessary for survival and recovery. The story of Kate demonstrates how traditional African values of communal healing can transform individual trauma into collective strength, resilience, and advocacy.

Kate's journey, as reported, began with what seemed like a blessing in disguise. After her father's death, her mother made the difficult decision to return to their ancestral village, leaving Kate in the care of her uncle so she could continue her education in town. With that arrangement, Kate could remain close to her friends, continue attending the school she was enroled in, and pursue her academic dreams without the disruption of relocation with her mother.

However, the safe space Kate had hoped for quickly transformed into a prison of fear and terror. Her uncle, the man entrusted with her care and protection, began subjecting her to sexual abuse. What started as inappropriate comments and unwanted touching escalated into more serious violations that left Kate feeling powerless and trapped. The very person who was supposed to shield her from harm became the source of her deepest trauma, creating a devastating betrayal of trust that would shake the foundations of her young world.

When Kate courageously attempted to seek help by confiding in her aunt about her husband's behaviour, she encountered another round of betrayal and silencing. Rather than offering protection or support, her aunt dismissed her concerns and joined her husband in threatening to send Kate back to the village if she continued to speak out.

Can you imagine?

Faced with the choice between enduring abuse and losing her educational opportunities, Kate felt cornered into silence, carrying her burden alone while watching her academic performance suffer under the weight of her trauma. Her situation extended far beyond the immediate physical violations she endured. Living in a household where her abuser held complete authority over her daily life meant that Kate existed in a constant state of fear and emotional torture.

Every interaction with her uncle was not without anxiety, as she tried to anticipate and avoid situations that might lead to abuse. The unpredictability of when violations might occur kept her nervous system in a perpetual state of activation, making it nearly impossible for her to relax, focus on her studies, or engage normally with her peers. Moreso, her uncle's position as a respected family member and community figure made it even more difficult for her to trust her perceptions of right and wrong, as the adult who should have been protecting her was instead exploiting her vulnerability.

Kate's academic decline reflected the cognitive impacts of trauma, as documented by researchers in the field. The constant stress of living with her abuser disrupted her ability to concentrate, retain information, and participate meaningfully in classroom activities. Teachers noticed her withdrawal and declining grades, but lacked the framework to understand these changes as potential indicators of abuse rather than simple academic struggles.

Cut off from her mother and extended family support system, threatened into silence by the very people who should have protected her, Kate found herself carrying an unbearable burden of trauma and isolation alone, at her very young age. This isolation not only intensified her trauma but also deprived her of communal support that traditionally helps African communities address and heal from situations like hers. The breakdown of protective family structures left Kate vulnerable not just to continued abuse, but to the secondary trauma of feeling abandoned and unsupported by her community.

Signs and Symptoms of Sexual Abuse & Exploitation
(in Kate's case)

The social worker from the Center for Clinical Care and Clinical Research Nigeria observed numerous indicators in Kate that aligned with documented signs of sexual abuse and exploitation. Her dramatic academic decline was one of the most noticeable changes, reflecting how trauma disrupts cognitive functioning and educational engagement. Research shows that children experiencing ongoing sexual abuse often struggle with concentration, memory retention, and academic motivation as their mental resources are consumed by hypervigilance and trauma processing (Kendall-Tackett et al., 1993).

Kate's social withdrawal became increasingly apparent to observant teachers and classmates. She had transformed from an engaged, social student into someone who avoided group activities, seemed reluctant to participate in class discussions, and appeared to carry a heavy emotional burden.

This social isolation is a common response to sexual abuse, as victims often feel different from their peers and fear that others will somehow discover their "shameful secret" (Finkelhor & Browne, 1985). Her withdrawal also served as a protective mechanism, as engaging with others felt risky and potentially exposing.

Physical manifestations of trauma were evident in Kate's presentation during the school workshop. The social worker noted her tense posture, the way she seemed to shrink into herself. These physical signs reflect the chronic stress response that develops when a child's nervous system is constantly activated by ongoing threat and trauma. Her body language communicated fear and alertness, which had become her default state.

Emotional dysregulation was another significant indicator observed in Kate's behavior. She experienced unpredictable mood swings, periods of intense sadness, and episodes of anger that seemed disproportionate to immediate circumstances. This emotional volatility is characteristic of trauma responses in children, as their developing emotional regulation systems become overwhelmed by experiences too intense to process normally. Research indicates that children who experience sexual abuse often struggle with emotional control as their nervous systems adapt to chronic stress (Cook et al., 2017).

Kate's reluctance to go home after school and her tendency to linger in safe spaces like the classroom reflected the fear and anxiety associated with her living situation. This habit of avoidance is common among children who are being abused in their homes, as they unconsciously seek to delay returning to environments where they feel unsafe. Teachers had noticed her hesitation to leave school grounds and her preference for staying busy with activities that kept her away from home

Her difficulty trusting new relationships and her initial hesitation to engage with the support group reflected the relational trauma she had experienced. Sexual abuse by a family member creates particular challenges with trust and attachment, as it violates the fundamental assumption that caregivers will provide safety and protection. Kate's cautious approach to new relationships showed both the wisdom she had developed about potential dangers and the barriers trauma had created to healthy connection and support.

Kate's Healing Journey

The intervention in Kate's case began when the Center for Clinical Care and Clinical Research Nigeria conducted an educational workshop at her school as part of their community outreach program. The social worker leading the team recognized the importance of creating awareness about sexual abuse within educational settings, understanding that schools often serve as the first point of contact where trained professionals might identify and support children and youth at risk. The workshop approach reflected an Afrocentric understanding that healing begins with community education and the creation of safe spaces for disclosure and support.

During the presentation on signs of abuse and mental health awareness, the social worker observed Kate's visible emotional response, noting how her body language changed as she appeared to recognize her own experiences in the descriptions being shared. This moment of recognition represented a crucial first step in Kate's healing journey, as it provided her with the language to understand that what she was experiencing was not normal or acceptable.

Following Kate's brave decision to approach the social worker after the session, the initial response prioritized validation and safety, recognizing that her willingness to disclose represented tremendous courage given her family's threats of abandonment. The social worker's immediate assurance that Kate was not alone and her invitation for ongoing support reflected core principles of Afrocentric healing, which emphasizes the restoration of connection and belonging as fundamental to recovery.

Introducing Kate to the Self-Reflection and Realization (SRAR) Support Group represented the implementation of a specifically Afrocentric healing model that draws on traditional African values of communal support and collective healing. This approach is hinged on the premise that individual trauma occurs within community contexts, and therefore requires community-based solutions. The decision to establish such groups within schools was also borne out of an understanding that educational institutions are natural community gathering places where healing could occur.

Weekly meetings in a welcoming classroom environment created a sense of consistency and safety in the healing journey, while the integration of outdoor activities and communal meals was reflective of African traditions of healing through connection with nature and shared nourishment. Research on African indigenous healing practices emphasizes the importance of group rituals, storytelling, and communal activities in processing trauma and restoring social connections (Nwoye, 2015).

The peer support aspect of the SRAR group proved particularly powerful for Kate's healing, as hearing other girls share similar experiences helped normalize her responses and reduce the isolation that trauma creates. This approach reflects the African philosophical concept of Ubuntu, which holds the view that individual healing occurs through community connection and mutual support. Research on group interventions for sexual abuse survivors shows that peer support can be particularly effective in reducing shame, building resilience, and developing healthy coping strategies (Hébert & Bergeron, 2007).

As Kate developed confidence within the support group, the social worker facilitated her gradual empowerment to advocate for herself within her family system, and for the first time, Kate spoke, and her uncle listened. The decision to arrange a facilitated family meeting reflected traditional African conflict resolution practices that bring the community together to address problems collectively rather than through adversarial approaches that might further fragment family relationships. The social worker's role as facilitator also draws on traditional African practices of community mediation, where respected community members help families handle conflicts and restore harmony in homes.

Ongoing support provided to Kate's uncle through counseling was done with the understanding that healing must occur at multiple levels within family and community systems. So, rather than simply removing Kate from the situation or focusing solely on punishment, the intervention created opportunities for the uncle to understand the impact of his actions and develop healthier ways of relating with Kate.

The transformation of Kate into a peer advocate and community leader is in line with the ultimate goal of Afrocentric healing approaches, which seek to turn individual trauma into collective strength and community wisdom. Her evolution from victim to survivor to advocate also aligns with the African philosophy that those who have experienced and overcome adversity have special responsibilities to support others facing similar challenges.

Kate's healing journey created ripple effects that challenged community silence around sexual abuse, while providing models for how families and communities can respond supportively to survivors.

The Role of Location, Culture, and Religion in Healing From Sexual Abuse/Exploitation

i) Indigenous Youth

From my observations, location plays a significant role in both risk and recovery. Indigenous youth in urban areas often face increased exposure to exploitative relationships and risky environments compared to those in remote or isolated regions, like the Arctic. In urban centers, youth are more likely to face peer pressure, exposure to unhealthy friendship circles, and a lack of close-knit community protections. In contrast, those in remote communities might have more cultural continuity but may also lack access to services.

The healing journey for Indigenous youth who have experienced sexual abuse and exploitation is deeply intertwined with their cultural identity, spiritual practices, and connection to community. Through my work, I have witnessed how the integration of traditional healing approaches alongside Western therapeutic methods creates powerful pathways to recovery. Ceremony is an essential part of traditional Native healing because physical and spiritual health are intimately connected, requiring body and spirit to heal together.

Indigenous healing practices recognize that trauma affects not just the individual but the entire community and ancestral connections. Indigenous Traditional Healing is a holistic practice that aims to treat imbalances in a person's body, mind, emotions, and spirit together. This understanding becomes particularly crucial when working with youth who have experienced sexual violence, as the trauma often disconnects them from their sense of self, community, and cultural identity.

The role of elders and traditional knowledge keepers cannot be overstated in the healing process. These community members provide not only guidance and mentorship but also serve as bridges between

38

traditional wisdom and contemporary healing needs. Their involvement helps restore the youth's sense of belonging and cultural continuity that trauma often disrupts. Traditional healing practices are localized and culturally specific, requiring cultural competence regarding the traditions and practices of any specific culture.

Location significantly impacts the healing process for Indigenous youth. Those in urban settings may struggle with cultural disconnection and lack of access to traditional healing resources, while those in remote communities might face challenges accessing comprehensive support services. However, each environment offers unique healing opportunities when approached with cultural sensitivity and community collaboration.

Let's consider a few case studies:

Nana (F)

Nana, a victim of sexual exploitation, required immediate attention to her most basic need, which was safety. Her trauma was deeply connected to specific locations where the abuse occurred, and that created complex triggers around environmental factors. Traditional approaches to safety planning needed to incorporate both her immediate physical needs and her cultural understanding of safe spaces.

Working within a housing-first model, I collaborated with Nana to identify not just any safe housing, but a culturally appropriate shelter that respected her Indigenous identity. We discussed what elements of home would support her healing, and ensured that her new housing was strategically located away from areas associated with her exploitation, but close to cultural resources and supportive community members.

Marie (F)

Marie presented with complex trauma from childhood parental sexual abuse, complicated by heavy substance use. However, her artistic talents and love for gallery exhibitions revealed a powerful pathway to healing. Her art became both her cultural expression and therapeutic outlet, connecting her to her Indigenous identity while processing trauma.

I worked with Marie to understand how her artistic practice connected to traditional Indigenous arts and storytelling. We explored how her contemporary gallery work could incorporate traditional symbols and themes, allowing her to reclaim her cultural narrative while addressing her trauma. Her artwork became a bridge between her pain and her cultural strength, transforming her gallery exhibitions from mere artistic expression to ceremonial acts of healing.

Supporting Marie's artistic journey meant advocating for cultural spaces where her work could be displayed and celebrated within Indigenous contexts. We connected her with Indigenous artist collectives and traditional art forms, and helped her understand her creativity as part of her cultural inheritance rather than separate from it. As her cultural identity strengthened through art, her reliance on substances decreased, and her sense of purpose and self-worth grew significantly.

Side Note:
When working with Indigenous youth who have experienced sexual abuse and exploitation, practitioners must recognize that culture is sometimes "medicinal" and integrate this understanding into all aspects of treatment. Healing approaches should carry along the youth's cultural identity while addressing their trauma. These elements cannot be separated without watering down the effectiveness of the healing process.

ii) Western Youth

The cultural setting of Western societies has a hand in how children and youths experience, express, and heal from sexual abuse and exploitation. Western culture's emphasis on individualism, self-reliance, and personal responsibility creates avenues for both opportunities and challenges in the healing process. These cultures are big on independence, autonomy, initiative and uniqueness, and also emphasise that individuals have the right and responsibility to look after themselves. This can sometimes lead to isolation during trauma recovery, but on the flipside, it also empowers the youth to take active roles in their healing journey.

In Western societies, therapeutic and healing practices are largely evidence-based. Trauma-focused therapies, especially cognitive behavioral therapy (CBT), are the primary treatment options for sexual abuse, with approaches like EMDR (Eye Movement Desensitization and Reprocessing), trauma-focused cognitive behavioral therapy, and psychodynamic therapy forming the foundation of treatment.

However, although only about 12% of the world's population lives in Western, educated, industrialized, and developed countries, over 80% of research findings come from these populations, which means Western therapeutic approaches are well-documented but may not always account for cultural diversity within Western societies themselves.

The role of location within Western cultures varies significantly between urban and rural settings. Urban environments often provide greater access to specialized services, diverse therapeutic options, and anonymity that some youth prefer when seeking help. However, these same environments can also present increased risk factors, including exposure to exploitation networks, substance availability, and social pressures. Rural Western communities may offer closer-knit support systems and less anonymity, but often struggle with limited resources, stigma, and reduced access to specialized trauma services.

Western culture's relationship with disclosure and help-seeking could be a bit complicated. While there are strong legal protections and professional systems in place to respond to sexual abuse, cultural factors such as privacy concerns, fear of family disruption, and stigma still create barriers to disclosure. The individualistic nature of Western society can sometimes leave youth feeling isolated in their trauma experience, lacking the community-based healing networks found in more collectivistic cultures.

The availability and accessibility of mental health services in Western societies is generally more extensive than in many other cultural contexts, yet barriers still exist. Insurance limitations, waitlists for specialized services, and the medicalized approach to trauma treatment can sometimes feel impersonal or overwhelming to children and youth. The Western emphasis on evidence-based practice ensures quality treatment but can sometimes overlook the need for culturally responsive approaches within diverse Western populations.

A brief case in point:

Judith (F)

In the course of working with a Western youth, let's call her Judith, I better appreciated the importance of personalizing healing approaches within Western treatment frameworks. Judith had Fetal Alcohol Spectrum Disorder (FASD) and had experienced childhood sexual abuse while remaining at risk for ongoing exploitation.

While I employed the same trauma-informed principles that guide my work with all clients, the delivery required significant adaptation to meet her unique cognitive and communication needs. Her case highlighted how Western healing approaches, while evidence-based and effective, must be flexible enough to accommodate diverse learning styles and cognitive capacities. In a nutshell, I was able to build the trust necessary for effective healing work through consistent and clear communication, and a client-centered approach.

Side Note:
Western emphasis on evidence-based healing practices ensure high-quality healing outcomes, but as social workers and health practitioners, we must remain flexible in our delivery methods to accommodate diverse learning styles, cognitive capacities, and individual needs. We must also be well aware that non-conventional expressions of trauma such as behavioural changes, substance use, or relationship difficulties are common and require patience on our end.

iii) Black/African Youth

Just as it is with Indigenous and Western youths, location also plays a crucial role in how young Blacks and Black Africans experience both trauma and healing. In rural locations dominated by most Blacks/Black Africans, for instance, the church might be the only safe space to process trauma.

At this point, we know that we cannot talk about healing for Black and African youths who have experienced sexual abuse and exploitation without considering the spiritual or religious side to it, because sometimes, we just have to meet people where they are, spiritually.

The truth is, most Black and African youths carry a unique burden when it comes to sexual trauma. They may be dealing with their personal pain while also facing racism, historical trauma, and cultural expectations that can make disclosure feel almost impossible. I've seen young people struggle with the weight of not wanting to speak up, or feeling like they're betraying their community by speaking up about abuse, especially when that abuse comes from within their family or community circles.

And these are the issues.

Most African-Americans would rather rely on their spiritual and religious communities for support in dealing with mental health issues rather than seeking professional help. But instead of labeling this as a barrier, we can see it as a strength to build upon. The Church has historically been a sanctuary, a place of healing, and a source of comfort that has sustained communities through centuries of adversity.

In African Christianity, I observe how many believers find strength in understanding their bodies as temples of the divine, deserving of reverence and protection. The emphasis on restoration rather than condemnation creates space for survivors to reclaim their spiritual identity without shame. Many African Christian communities practice collective prayer and laying on of hands, thereby creating a supportive environment where survivors can experience divine love through human community.

I have heard many Black folks say that they rely on prayer to help make major decisions, and this doesn't change when they're dealing with trauma. In fact, it often intensifies. I've sat with young people who have been through abuse, and who expressed their belief in God to heal them.

Some of them asked to pray over certain aspects of their healing, and that is very okay. These aren't conversations you can have without understanding the profound role that faith plays in the identity of these individuals, and their healing, by extension.

In this context, the role of the church leader or spiritual leader becomes crucial. When young people who have experienced sexual abuse can connect with pastors, church mothers, or spiritual mentors who understand trauma and can provide theologically sound support, the healing process will accelerate dramatically. These are the people who can help survivors find themselves, know their worth, and connect them to the source of their divinity.

Healing in Black and African communities is beautifully interesting, if I should put it that way. Concepts of healing in the Black community are a bit complex and raise many critical issues, particularly around gender roles and expectations.

Young Black women often carry the additional burden of being seen as "strong" and expected to endure and overcome without complaint. Young Black men face the challenge that boys, particularly Black boys, are raised to believe that expressing their emotions or being vulnerable is a sign of weakness.

Further from the Christian faith, Traditional African healing has been in existence for many centuries, and has proven to be effective. Many Black and African youths practice daily meditation and engage in mindfulness practices, and these systems are all pathways to healing. I have seen many youths encounter healing through this route.

The community aspect cannot be overstated. African-Americans tend to rely on informal sources of support such as the church, clergy, friends, and family. Healing happens in beauty salons, at church social functions, mosques, in Sunday school classes, and around family dinner tables. As social workers, we must acknowledge this.

As we conclude, here's the story of Annie, an African youth who survived trauma and became an advocate, thanks to the power of her community.

Annie (F)

Annie's story began in tragedy. Her childhood was stolen through gang rape, and as if that was not enough, her uncle continued the cycle of abuse in her adolescent years, thereby destroying her ability to trust even family. As a teenager, she had another experience of gang rape and this accumulated weight of repeated trauma brought Annie to her breaking point.

Her desperate cry for help became her salvation. Annie's friends rallied around, and through their efforts, a Non-Governmental Organization discovered her story and reached out immediately, recognizing the urgent need for intervention. Initially hesitant, Annie agreed to meet with the team and eventually joined the support group for survivors of sexual and gender-based violence.

The support group became Annie's lifeline. Week after week, she gathered with other women who understood her pain intimately. Through art therapy, she began expressing emotions she had buried for decades, painting and drawing her way through trauma. The group practiced self-care strategies together – journaling, meditation, and mindfulness exercises that helped Annie focus on the present rather than being haunted by her past.

Within this circle of understanding, Annie learned to set boundaries and rebuild trust, not just in others, but in herself. The women became her sisters, offering the family connection that trauma had severed. With this consistent therapeutic support and newfound bonds, Annie discovered her own worth and recognized the strength she had always possessed.

Annie's transformation from victim to survivor to advocate inspired countless young women in her community. Her courage in sharing her story publicly broke the silence that often surrounds sexual abuse, showing others that healing was possible even after the darkest experiences. She had not only survived against all odds, but had embraced a life filled with hope and purpose. Her past remained part of her story, but it no longer controlled her future. She had become a beacon of resilience, demonstrating the unwavering strength of the human spirit and the healing power of community support.

Side Note:
The community-centered nature of healing in Black and African cultures means that individual therapy, while important, must be balanced with community support and spiritual guidance. The isolation that often comes with trauma is particularly harmful in cultures where identity and healing are inherently communal experiences.

Location, religion, and culture truly matter, and as social workers, it is our responsibility to not isolate them, but see them as complementing systems that are instrumental to complete healing of sexually abused and exploited children and youth.

Reflections & Conclusion

Apart from the signs of sexual abuse mentioned in the stories above, I have observed that survivors frequently begin avoiding certain people and past pleasurable experiences, as these may trigger traumatic memories or create feelings of vulnerability they are not ready to face. Parents and caregivers are encouraged to be sensitive, and watch out for neighbors, distant relatives, or any individual their wards may not be comfortable around.

Changes in walking posture and general body movements are common. Survivors may become more guarded in how they carry themselves, walking with shoulders hunched or avoiding eye contact, as their bodies unconsciously try to make themselves less visible or approachable.

The development of timidity and shyness often emerges as survivors struggle with trust and self-confidence, particularly in situations that once felt comfortable. Additionally, incoherence in speech can manifest as survivors may dissociate during conversations or find themselves unable to articulate their thoughts clearly, especially when discussing anything that might relate to their trauma. Parents, caregivers and educators should pay attention to these gestures.

There may be sudden changes in academic or work performance, unexplained knowledge of sexual topics inappropriate for their age (particularly in children), or regression to earlier developmental behaviors. Physical symptoms might include unexplained injuries (especially in pubic regions), frequent urinary tract infections, or psychosomatic complaints like headaches and stomach problems. Educators, especially, must be observant of young people in this category, and communicate their observations to parents or caregivers.

Some survivors develop eating disorders as a way to regain control over their bodies, while others may engage in self-harm behaviors or exhibit age-inappropriate sexual behavior. Changes in personal hygiene (either becoming obsessively clean or neglecting self-care entirely) can also be a significant indicator.

Parents and stakeholders are encouraged to be actively present in the lives of these young ones, so as to spot any of these anomalies, and respond appropriately.

CHAPTER THREE
HEALING PATH FOR GRIEVING CHILDREN & YOUTH

"Healing from grief does not end in returning to who you were before the trauma, it is only complete when you have become who you are meant to be because of it." - Eseosa Omoregie

Most people say that you don't know what you have until you lose it, but I dare to ask if that really holds true. Well, that might be true, but what happens when the very person or thing you so much cherish, probably worked your entire life for, slips through your palms and goes with the wind?

Have you ever watched a young loved one struggle helplessly for life, and eventually surrender to the cold hands of death, right before you? Or let's assume you weren't there. How did it feel when the news got to

Have you been so careful about a business move or transaction, trusting your guts that all will be well, then suddenly, disaster struck, and in a matter of minutes, you go from plenty to penury? Did life remain the same after any such or similar experience?

I am sure you have answers, but I cannot receive them here. However, answers made available from research by Amerispeak and WebMD show that 57% of Americans are grieving the loss of someone close to them over the last three years. That means every other person you meet is dealing with grief, and to be honest, grief never really goes away completely.

The truth is, loss changes us at the deepest level. When we experience significant loss, our brains literally have to rewire themselves and learn new patterns of thinking and being. As one researcher puts it, grieving is a form of learning, and we have to learn new rules for navigating a world that suddenly feels weird without the person or thing we've lost.

Grief can take many forms, especially for children and youth. It is not limited to the loss of a loved one. Grief can manifest in different ways: the loss of a parent, the loss of one's identity, the absence of support, or even the inability to achieve a specific goal.

As human beings, we have the capacity to process grief. Elisabeth Kübler-Ross, a renowned grief theorist, introduced a model that outlines five stages of grief: denial, anger, bargaining, depression, and acceptance. However, not everyone moves through all these stages, and some may never fully reach the stage of acceptance. It's important to recognize that grief is a process, not a metric. Each person's journey through grief is unique. Some process it quickly, while others may never fully overcome it.

In many children and youth, grief often manifests during the anger phase. This can be expressed through negative behavior or hostility toward themselves and others in their social circles. Many young people struggle to process their grief and may not know how to express or release their anger healthily.

Let us quickly consider the five stages of grief, as put together by Dr. Elisabeth Kübler-Ross

Stage 1: Denial

Denial is your mind's way of protecting you from overwhelming shock and buying you time to slowly absorb reality at a pace you can handle. For young people, denial might look like continuing to talk about a deceased relative as though they are still alive, or setting a place at the table for someone who has died. This stage isn't permanent, and you shouldn't rush through it. Fighting against denial too hard can make it last longer. Instead, gently acknowledge these feelings and let them naturally fade when your mind is ready to handle reality.

Stage 2: Anger

When denial begins to crack, anger often rushes in, and it can get intense depending on the individual's temperament. You might find yourself furious at the person who died, at God, at yourself, or even at innocent people around you. This anger can feel frightening, especially if you usually consider yourself calm and controlled. For young people, this might mean being angry at friends whose parents are still alive, but this anger isn't really about these targets, but the unfairness of loss itself.

Stage 3: Bargaining

Bargaining is your mind's attempt to regain control when you feel utterly powerless. It's the "what if" and "if only" stage, where you become convinced you can somehow reverse the loss through negotiation. For children and teens, bargaining might involve repenting from their wrongdoings, making promises to be perfect, or refusing to sleep in their bed because staying in a deceased parent's room feels like it keeps them connected. While these thoughts might seem irrational, they show the capacity of these young minds to keep fighting even when the battle seems lost.

Stage 4: Depression

When bargaining fails and reality fully sets in, depression often follows. The difference between this kind of depression and clinical depression is that it is situational, appropriate, and ultimately healing (though it might be an awful experience). During this stage, the mind does an important work of reorganizing our entire internal world, and learns to exist without that person or thing that was so important to us. For young people, this might mean losing interest in activities they once loved, or becoming unnecessarily clingy.

Stage 5: Acceptance

Acceptance doesn't necessarily mean one has gotten over the loss or that they have stopped caring. Instead, it means they have learned to carry their loss in a way that allows them to live again. In this stage, the sharp edges of grief begin to smooth out. We find ourselves able to think about our loved ones without being overwhelmed by pain. We may even smile at memories instead of only crying. For young people, acceptance might mean being able to talk about their loss without breaking down, or being able to form new relationships without feeling like they are betraying the person they lost.

***

Having laid this foundation for the understanding of grief and its stages, let us consider a number of grief-related cases and their healing journeys from the following perspectives:

Indigenous Perspective on Grief

Indigenous cultures often approach grief in a communal manner, viewing it as a collective experience where family and community members support one another throughout the healing process. Spiritual connections, rituals, and ceremonies play a central role in helping individuals connect with lost loved ones, as well as with the land and ancestors. This communal and spiritual approach to grief is integral to many Indigenous belief systems.

(Emily's Story)

I worked with a youth at a group home, which I'll refer to as Emily. Emily had an outgoing personality and was very sociable, but she displayed extreme aggression toward her peers and even the staff members. Emily had a history of childhood abuse, including witnessing domestic violence, as well as early exposure to drugs and alcohol. She was apprehended by child protective services as she approached her teenage years and moved through several foster homes before finding a permanent placement at the group home.

Over time, as we developed a relationship built on trust, I began to realize that Emily was grieving the separation from her parents. Her aggression was a result of her inability to fully process the grief from her childhood trauma at the time of her apprehension. Recognizing this, I worked with her on understanding her emotions and finding healthy ways to express and release her anger. We talked about the fact that healing is a process and that it's okay if some people never fully reach the acceptance stage of grief. I helped Emily understand that grieving doesn't necessarily mean letting go completely, but it is about learning to live with the loss in a healthier way.

One of the most empowering things for grieving children is helping them understand that grief is a personal journey. Building a relationship with them, not just as a professional, but as someone who can empathize with their pain, can help. Children need to feel that they are not just being pitied, but understood. In Emily's case, her strength was music and sometimes dancing. She was excellent in music, and she was able to channel her emotions through this form.

Emily related better as time went on with staff and even her housemates, this also reflected in her commitment to activities and goals. Though she was still struggling with alcohol use, the instances were minimized. Over time, Emily learned to process her grief, her anger decreased, and she began to build healthier relationships with her peers both at home and at school. Emily later secured a volunteer placement within the organization.

Signs and Symptoms of Grief *(in Emily's Story)*

The first sign we can observe from Emily's story was that her grief was layered with childhood trauma. She had witnessed domestic violence and been exposed to drugs and alcohol early in her life. When child protective services stepped in as she approached her teenage years, she found herself moving through several foster homes before landing at the group home. Each transition likely reopened old wounds.

Another sign to pay attention to was Emily's aggression which was a clear indication of her inability to fully process the grief from her childhood trauma, at the time of her apprehension. She was grieving the separation from her parents.

Emily was also struggling with alcohol use, which often becomes a way for people to numb emotional pain when they don't have other tools to cope. Her difficulties weren't just about missing her parents, they were about processing a whole childhood of loss, trauma, and broken trust.

Emily's Healing Journey

The first step in Emily's healing journey was helping her understand her emotions, and finding healthy ways to express and release her anger. I also helped her acknowledge that healing is a process, and that it's okay if some people never fully reach the acceptance stage of grief.

One of the most important realizations in Emily's journey was understanding that grieving doesn't necessarily mean letting go completely, but learning to live with the loss in a healthier way. This reframing of the mind was important because it gave Emily the permission to still care about her parents while also moving forward with her life.

Emily's strength turned out to be music and sometimes dancing. She was excellent at music, and she was able to channel her emotions through this form of expression. This became a beautiful route to healing in her case, as it aided the processing of feelings that were too big for words.

Though Emily still struggled with alcohol use, the instances were minimized over time. Small victories started adding up. She began relating better with staff and even her housemates, and this improvement reflected in her commitment to activities and her goals. As Emily learned to process her grief, her anger decreased naturally. She began building healthier relationships with her peers both at home and at school, and the aggression that had once defined her interactions began to fade as she found better ways to communicate her needs and feelings.

The most beautiful part of Emily's healing journey was when she secured a volunteer placement within the organization. This was an act of giving back, but beyond that, she found and immersed herself in a community that had helped her heal. Isn't it beautiful to see someone go from needing professional support, to someone who could offer support to others? That's the beauty of healing.

One of the things I deeply respect about Indigenous cultures is their holistic approach to life and healing. Their principles, deeply rooted in connection to the land, community, and ancestors, are both unique and profound.

In terms of grief, one particular belief that stands out to me is the teaching of the turtle, which is part of the Seven Teachings in many First Nations cultures. The turtle is often seen as a symbol of life itself, embodying patience, stability, and a deep connection to the Earth. This teaching reminds us that healing is a slow and steady process, and that we must be patient with ourselves and with each other as we navigate the journey of grief.

Here's the story of another youth I worked with in an outreach setting, let's name her Zoe.

(Zoe's Story)

Zoe had been separated from her single mother at birth due to her mother's legal issues. She never had the chance to meet her mother, and when Zoe became a teenager, she learned of her mother's passing. This news marked the beginning of Zoe's grief journey, which persisted throughout her childhood.

She often expressed her grief through isolation, withdrawing from others, and becoming less sociable with her peers. Zoe struggled to set and achieve goals, and she lacked motivation to pursue anything in her life.

One of the few things Zoe found solace in was her spiritual connection. She developed a relationship with an elder, a respected community member who guided her spiritually and culturally. This connection seemed to provide her with a sense of stability and purpose.

Additionally, Zoe participated in drumming activities, which helped her release some of her grief. The act of drumming allowed her to channel her emotions, serving as both an outlet and a form of healing. I observed firsthand how Zoe's connection to her culture and spirituality supported her emotional well-being, especially in the face of significant loss.

Signs of Grief *(in Zoe's Story)*

The genesis of Zoe's heartbreaking situation was the separation from her single mother at birth, due to her mother's legal issues. She never had the chance to meet her mother, not even once. Can you imagine growing up with that kind of absence? It's like mourning someone who was both everything and nothing to you at the same time.

When Zoe became a teenager, she learned of her mother's passing. That news hit hard, and it marked the beginning of what I could see was going to be a long, complicated grief journey. The thing about losing someone you never knew is that it closes the door on possibilities forever. There would never be a reunion, never be answers to the questions that had probably kept her awake at night.

Zoe's grief also manifested in ways that were easy to miss if you weren't paying close attention. She often expressed her grief through isolation, pulling away from anyone who tried to get close. She became less sociable with her peers, and I watched her withdraw deeper and deeper into herself. It was like she was disappearing right in front of us.

The lack of motivation was another telling sign. Zoe struggled to set and achieve goals, and she seemed to lack any drive to pursue anything in her life. I wouldn't call that laziness. I'd rather infer that she couldn't see the point in trying when the most important relationship in her life had been taken from her before it even began.

Zoe's Healing Journey

Zoe's journey to healing was deeply personal, and rooted in something much more profound than traditional therapy approaches. Her healing began when she found her spiritual connection, and honestly, watching it unfold was one of the most beautiful things I've witnessed in my work.

The turning point came when Zoe developed a relationship with an elder, a respected community member who guided her spiritually and culturally. It was like she had found the missing piece of herself. The elder didn't try to fix her or tell her to get over her grief. Instead, they helped her understand her place in something bigger than her individual pain. This connection seemed to provide Zoe with a sense of stability and purpose that she had been missing her entire life. For the first time, I saw her begin to lift her head up and engage with the world around her confidently.

The drumming activities became another crucial part of her healing journey. The act of drumming allowed her to channel her emotions in her unique way, and also serve as both an outlet and a form of healing, giving her a way to express all the grief she had been carrying inside. It is safe to assume that through the drums, she could speak to her mother in a way she never could in life. She could express her anger, her sadness, her longing. All of it poured out through her hands into those drums.

Slowly, I watched Zoe begin to emerge from her isolation. She started engaging more with her peers naturally, as someone who had found her footing again. Her healing journey is testament to the fact that sometimes, healing happens through trans-human connection to something bigger than ourselves. Zoe found her way back to life through drums and spirituality, thanks to the elder who led her through that transformation.

Afrocentric Perspective on Grief

Similar to the Indigenous model, healing within the Afrocentric setting tells us that grief is not merely an individual experience but a communal one, deeply rooted in the understanding that we are interconnected beings whose pain and healing ripple through the entire community. Therefore, Afrocentric healing approaches categorizes grief as a natural human response that requires collective support, storytelling, and spiritual grounding to navigate successfully.

(Anna's Story, as reported by a social worker in Africa)

When Anna was just 13, her world shattered. In two short years, she lost both of her parents. Her father, a police officer, died after a brief illness, leaving her mother one month pregnant. Eight months later, her mother delivered a baby boy and died three months after birth. The laughter that once filled her home disappeared, leaving a heavy silence that echoed through her life. She and her younger siblings had to relocate to her maternal aunt's house.

At first, she was in shock. How could this happen? Her parents had always been her support system. Now, at such a young age, she felt completely lost. Friends would ask how she was doing, and she'd force a smile, saying, "I'm fine" while inside she felt empty.

As time passed, the weight of her grief became harder to carry. Anna often withdrew from her friends and activities she once enjoyed. The happy girl who loved to dance and laugh was now a shadow of herself. She spent hours alone in her room, battling with feelings of sadness and confusion.

Although her aunt was playing the motherly role perfectly well, Anna still wasn't emotionally fine, and this played out in her academic performance. She performed academically low. Nothing excited her anymore, and she was always depressed. She was taken through counseling sessions in school, but it felt difficult to open up. She thought, "Who would really understand what I'm going through?"

At 17, Anna found herself reflecting on her journey. She took a step she never thought she would. She opened up to someone who introduced her to a trauma consciousness therapist and a grief support group. The first day, she felt nervous. Walking into a room full of strangers, she wondered if sharing her story would help.

But then, something surprising happened. As she listened to others speak about their losses, she realized she wasn't alone. She heard stories that were even more grieving than hers. Someone shared a story of losing both parents and two siblings to a car accident, leaving only him in this cruel world. Then she realized that the room was filled with people who understood and related to her pain. When it was her turn to share, the words poured out.

She talked about her parents, their love, and how much she missed them. For the first time, she felt a weight lift. It was her first step in the healing process.

In one of the group sessions, they were encouraged to create memory boxes. Anna loved the idea. She gathered pictures, letters, and little things that reminded her of her parents. Each item held a story, a piece of her heart.

As she crafted her memory box, she felt a shift inside. Instead of just mourning their loss, she began to celebrate their lives. She remembered the family gatherings, the holidays filled with laughter, and the lessons they taught her. Anna started journaling her thoughts, which became a powerful outlet. Writing about her feelings helped her process the grief instead of burying it. She learned that it was okay to feel sad, but she could also find joy in the memories of her parents.

Now, at 19, she uses her experience to help others. She volunteers with organizations that support grieving youth, sharing her story to inspire hope. "Talking about grief can break the silence," she believes, and it helps others feel less alone.

Anna knows that grief doesn't have a set timeline. There are still days when the loss feels fresh, but she has learned to embrace her parents' memory. She celebrates their lives during special occasions, keeping their spirit alive in her heart.

Her journey has shown her that while grief can change you, it doesn't have to define you. Anna continues to find joy in life, carrying her parents' love with her, and inspiring others to do the same.

Signs and Symptoms of Grief *(in Anna's Story)*

The initial shock Anna experienced was her mind's way of protecting itself from the overwhelming reality of losing both parents within two years. This numbness served as a temporary shield, but it also created a disconnect between her inner reality and the face she presented to the world.

Her withdrawal from friends and activities she once enjoyed revealed how grief had robbed her of the connections that typically sustain young people. The happy girl who loved to dance and laugh becoming a shadow of herself showed how grief can literally diminish one's sense of self. Anna spent hours alone in her room, battling with feelings of sadness and confusion, demonstrating how grief often drives us into isolation when we most need connection.

The academic decline was another significant indicator of how deeply her grief had affected her. Despite her aunt's loving care, Anna's emotional state manifested in her inability to concentrate or engage with her studies. The pervasive depression and loss of interest in activities that once brought joy are classic signs of complicated grief, particularly when it occurs during critical developmental years.

Perhaps most telling was Anna's difficulty opening up during school counseling sessions. Her thought, "Who would really understand what I'm going through?" reflected the isolation that grief can create, making sufferers feel uniquely alone in their pain. This sense of being misunderstood is particularly acute for young people who may feel that their peers cannot relate to such profound loss.

Anna's Healing Journey

Anna's healing journey began the moment she realized she wasn't alone. Hearing others share stories of their losses, and recognizing that the room was filled with people who understood her pain reflects the Afrocentric understanding that healing happens through connection and collective witnessing. Her ability to finally share her story and feel "a weight lift" tells us how speaking one's truth within a supportive community can begin the healing process.

The creation of memory boxes (which is an Afrocentric healing practice) helped her form some sort of connection with her late parents who had transitioned. Rather than focusing solely on the loss, Anna began to celebrate her parents' lives, reminiscing on the family gatherings, holidays filled with laughter, and the lessons they taught her.

We also see how journaling and storytelling helped Anna process grief, rather than hide it. This practice of expressing internal experiences through creative means, is consistent with African traditions of storytelling as a means of healing and finding meaning. As she consistently expressed her experiences through writing, she learned to hold space for both sad and joyful experiences. Her decision to volunteer with organizations supporting grieving youths and share her story to inspire hope reflects the African concept of Ubuntu—the idea that we are all connected and that our individual healing contributes to the healing of the community.

Most importantly, Anna's healing journey shows that while grief can change us, it doesn't have to define us. Her ability to find joy in life while carrying her parents' love with her reflects the Afrocentric understanding that healing involves learning to live fully while immortalizing those who have transitioned. Her story inspires others to do the same, and encourages the cycle of communal healing which is a key Afrocentric approach to grief and loss.

(Ken's Story, as reported by a social worker in Africa)

What happens to a nine-year-old boy's heart when the man who taught him how to throw a ball, who carried him on his shoulders, who promised to always be there, simply... disappears? Ken was just 9 years old when his life took a painful turn that would reshape everything he thought he knew about love, security, and what it means to be a man.

His father left, abandoning him, his mother, and his siblings to start a new life with someone else. Growing up, Ken and his siblings had always looked up to their dad. They shared great moments—playing together, going out on adventures, watching movies curled up on the couch. They never lacked anything, not just materially, but emotionally too. His father had been their hero, their protector, their example of what a man should be.

But after his father left, those happy memories felt like daggers to the heart. What do you do with the good memories when the person who created them has caused you the deepest pain? Life became hard for Ken and his siblings as his mother couldn't take care of their financial needs because his father had always been their financial backbone. In that moment, Ken felt a deep sense of rejection and lack. It was as if a part of him was missing, and not just any part, but the part that told him he was worthy of love.

At school and even in church, he tried to act normal, but inside, he was struggling. Even in sacred spaces where he should have felt comfort, he still felt lonely. He often sat by himself, feeling like nobody understood what he was going through. Perhaps most damaging of all, he began to hate father figures, believing they were wicked beings just like his father. How could he trust any man when the one who was supposed to love him unconditionally had walked away so easily?

After secondary school, at age 16, life got tougher. He had to leave the town where they stayed to go hustle in another, so he could support his mother and younger sibling. Here was a teenage boy, carrying the weight of a man's responsibilities, trying to fill the void his father had left behind.

Signs and Symptoms of Grief (in Ken's Story)

Ken's grief showed up in ways that were both visible and hidden, like an iceberg with most of its mass beneath the surface. The most obvious sign was his deep sense of rejection and lack (feeling like a part of him was missing). This wasn't just sadness, but a fundamental questioning of his worth as a person. When the man who was supposed to love you unconditionally walks away, what does that say about your value?

His hatred of father figures revealed how deeply the abandonment had wounded him. Ken had generalized his father's betrayal to all men in positions of authority or care, believing they were "wicked beings" just like his father. This kind of categorical thinking is common in grief. The mind tries to protect itself from future hurt by building walls against anything that reminds us of our pain.

The loneliness that followed him everywhere, even into sacred spaces like church, showed how grief had isolated him from the very communities that should have offered comfort. He would sit by himself, feeling like nobody understood what he was going through. This isolation wasn't just about being alone physically, it was about feeling fundamentally different from everyone around him, marked by a pain that seemed impossible to explain.

Let's not forget how he tried to act normal at school and church while struggling inside. This masking behavior is incredibly common among grieving children and teenagers, who often feel pressure to appear "fine" while carrying enormous emotional burdens. Ken was performing normally, while his inner world was falling apart.

The financial pressure that forced him to leave home at 16 to fend for himself in a different city showed how his father's abandonment had practical consequences that extended far beyond the emotional realm. Ken wasn't just grieving a relationship, but his childhood, his security, and his right to simply be a teenager.

Ken's Healing Journey

One day at the church he joined, Ken met a young man named Samuel, who had also faced loss. Samuel had lost both his parents at a young age and understood the pain Ken was feeling. He reached out to Ken and talked about the Self Reflection and Realization (SRAR) Corner, a special support group in the form of a picnic, organized by an Adolescent girls and young person's advocate, Astar.

Ken decided to join. The first time he attended, he was amazed by the warm atmosphere. Surrounded by nature, the setting felt peaceful and inviting (a stark contrast to the chaos that had become his inner world). At the SRAR picnic, people gathered to share their stories in a relaxed environment. They enjoyed food, laughter, and the beauty of nature. Hearing others talk about their struggles made Ken realize he wasn't alone. He shared his own story too, and it felt good to connect with people who understood his pain.

During the picnic, they engaged in trauma-relieving activities like experience sharing, art therapy, and sound therapy. During the experience sharing, each person was handed a blank piece of paper, a powerful symbol that there was still a page in their life that they could decide to fill with happy memories, even though the other pages were filled with sadness.

During the art therapy, Ken picked up a paintbrush and started to express his feelings through drawings. Each stroke helped him process his sadness while finding joy in creativity. It brought back tears and memories, but one could see that healing had started. The tears didn't take long to dry as he could feel the pain of others too, reassuring him that his case wasn't the worst.

As the weeks went by, Ken started to heal. He learned that it was okay to feel sad and angry, but he also discovered the importance of finding joy in life. He learned how to see fathers as nurturing figures rather than wicked ones. He had male mentors who served as father figures in his life. The mentor at the SRAR Corner taught him how to be resilient and helped him rebuild his confidence. Ken began to open up more about his experiences. Each time he shared his story, it felt like a weight lifted off his shoulders. The friends he made at the SRAR picnics became like family, and they reminded him that he was worthy of love and support.

Now, at 19, Ken is on a new path. He was introduced to Blockchain Technology through a tech boot-camp that was organized by SRAR in partnership with his church. Ken now earns in dollars, and is doing well for himself, even as a teenager. While he still feels lonely sometimes, he has learned how to cope. He has strong friendships and a support network that he can rely on.

Perhaps most remarkably, he went ahead to reach out to his father, whom life had dealt with harshly. He sends his father money sometimes. This is someone he had vowed never to come in contact with again, but healing had transformed his heart in ways he never imagined possible.

He has learned that healing isn't a destination but a journey, and that community makes all the difference. His transformation from a broken nine-year-old to a successful, compassionate young man shows that while abandonment can wound us deeply, it doesn't have to define us. Ken chose to write a different ending to his story, and in doing so, he became living proof that healing is always possible.

Before we conclude this chapter, let us consider healing from grief, from a Western perspective.

Western Perspective on Grief

Have you ever wondered how some people seem to carry their pain, not as a burden, but as something that has moulded them into who they were meant to become? You will find the story of this lady interesting, and inspiring at the same time. She was humbled by loss, but would humble grief years later and share her story. For the purpose of anonymity, let's call this lady Eliana.

(Eliana's Story)

The lady, Eliana, was raised in a decent and well-to-do family where everything pretty much went well. Her family did not lack any good thing, and she had the best education available at the time. Life was comfortable and safe, more like the kind of childhood that feels like it would last forever.

But at the age of ten, life, like most people would say, happened to Eliana's household. They suffered a major loss, and that plunged the entire family into a state of economic crisis. Everything seemed to take a drastic turn, as they went from plenty to penury. Life was truly hard for Eliana, and for the first time, at that tender age, she cried bitterly. Can you imagine being ten years old and watching your entire world crumble?

Eliana managed to grow through the pain into her twenties, carrying that early lesson about life's unpredictability like a scar that had never quite healed. And then, tragedy struck again. She lost her mother, but this time, something interesting happened.

When she was faced with the loss of her mom, she didn't run from it. The fact that she had experienced the effects of loss and pain right from infancy made her get to the acceptance stage of grief quickly. Of course, she did mourn the demise of her late mother, but she did not collapse or feel broken. Something had shifted in her the first time she saw life really tear someone down, so she learned at that early stage that strength is not necessarily the absence of pain, but the ability to live through it.

And in living through the pain, Eliana vowed to be the kind of person who helps others stand when life tries to knock them over. Not because she is stronger, but because she has tasted and understood sorrow, and has felt the silence that follows loss. She has known what it means to wake up and wish she hadn't, and that had greatly unearthed the empathy in her, and contributed to her pace of healing.

She submitted herself to mentorship, Dialectical Behaviour Therapy, and intentional personal development. Today, Eliana has built a profitable career for herself, expresses herself more through creativity, and now trains many other young individuals on different sets of skills. Having fully healed from the trauma of her childhood and adulthood losses, Eliana has been careful not to write anyone off in life. She sees potential even in pain, strength in scars, and holds the view that sometimes, the most broken people carry the deepest wisdom and the loudest silence.

Reflections From Eliana's Healing Journey

What stands out for me in Eliana's healing journey is what Western psychology would call post-traumatic growth, that is the idea that people can emerge from trauma not just intact, but actually stronger and more capable than before. Her path to healing wasn't about forgetting her pain or pretending it didn't happen, but it was about integrating it into her identity in a way that served both her and others.

Her decision to submit herself to mentorship, Dialectical Behavior Therapy, and personal development highlights a Western approach to healing that is big on individual agency and professional intervention. DBT, in particular, is designed to help people develop skills for managing intense emotions and building resilience—exactly what Eliana needed to process her relationship with loss.

What makes Eliana's healing even more beautiful is how she transformed her understanding of strength itself. She learned that strength is not the absence of pain, but the ability to live through it. This reframing is in line, and even central to many Western therapeutic approaches that say that we can change our relationship with our experiences even when we can't change the experiences themselves.

Her vow to help others stand when life tries to knock them over wasn't born from a place of superiority or having "gotten over" her pain. Instead, it came from what Western psychology calls "wounded healer" syndrome—the idea that our deepest wounds can become our greatest sources of wisdom and compassion.

What about the creativity that became part of her healing process? That is still in line with the Western view that artistic expression can be a powerful tool for processing trauma and finding meaning. Through creative expression, Eliana found a way to transform her internal experience into something external, something that could be shared, understood, and appreciated by others. Her success in building a profitable career and training other young individuals also shows that rather than soak in grief perpetually, she channeled her youthful energy into mastering her craft, and as a result, created value that was needed and rewarded.

In the course of her healing journey, she learned not to write anyone off in life, to see potential even in pain, and strength in scars. Her belief that "sometimes, the most broken people carry the deepest wisdom and the loudest silence" also reveals a major philosophical shift in her mindset, one that can only be expressed by one who has truly healed.

Side Note: Healing from grief (from a Western perspective) does not end in returning to who you were before the trauma, it is only complete when you have become who you are meant to be because of it. The fact that she has fully healed doesn't mean she's forgotten her losses or that they no longer affect her. Instead, it means she's integrated them into her life story in a way that serves her growth and allows her to serve others. Finally, her healing is complete not because her pain is gone, but because she has learned to carry it with grace and use it as a source of strength rather than a source of limitation.

Reflections & Conclusion

I have observed that children and young people experiencing loss and grief often display moodiness and mood swings that can seem unpredictable and intense. One moment they might appear fine, laughing with friends, and the next they might burst into tears or become irritable over seemingly minor issues. These emotional fluctuations express the internal struggle of processing loss, as their minds work to make sense of a reality that has been distorted. Parents and caregivers should understand that these mood changes are normal responses to grief and not necessarily signs of behavioral problems.

Isolation is another common response I have witnessed, where grieving children and youth begin withdrawing from family, friends, and activities they once enjoyed. They may spend excessive time alone in their rooms, decline invitations to social events, or seem emotionally distant even when physically present. This withdrawal often stems from feeling that others cannot understand their pain, or from a fear that engaging with the world might somehow mean they're "moving on" from their loved one. Educators and family members should be patient with this tendency while gently encouraging connection when appropriate.

Every adult who comes in contact with grieving children carries a responsibility to create an enabling environment where they feel safe to process their pain without judgment or pressure to suddenly overcome it. The stories shared reveal that there's no one-size-fits-all approach to supporting grieving children, therefore we must expand our understanding of what healing looks like, bearing in mind that what works for one child may not work for another.

And to the survivor reading this, I see you. You are strong and I admire the strength and courage you have put up despite your loss and the grief that came with it. Your healing journey won't look like anyone else's, and that's okay. Some days you might find comfort in talking to someone who understands, whether that's a counselor, a friend, or a support group where others share your pain. Other days, you might heal through creating something (music, art, writing, or any form of expression that helps you process what words can't capture).

Don't be afraid to lean into your cultural or spiritual practices if they bring you peace, and remember that it's okay to have good days and bad days, sometimes within the same hour. Most importantly, please don't isolate yourself completely. I know it feels safer sometimes, but healing happens in connection, even when that connection feels scary.

Find small ways to contribute to your community or help others when you're ready, because your pain, as terrible as it feels right now, can become a source of strength and wisdom that helps both you and others heal. You don't have to rush this process, you don't have to get over the ugly experiences by any timeline, and you don't have to pretend you're okay when you're not. Just take it one breath, one day, one small step at a time, and you will be fine.

CHAPTER FOUR
HEALING FOR CHILDREN & YOUTH IN CONFLICT WITH THE LAW

"Supporting youth in conflict with the law requires a deep understanding of their past experiences, and the ways in which trauma has shaped their behavior." - Eseosa Omoregie

When we talk about youth in conflict with the law, we are referring to young individuals who have been involved in criminal activities, or have violated legal boundaries and are now under probation or some form of supervision due to these charges. Understanding the background and history of these youth is crucial in addressing their needs, and supporting their rehabilitation.

Working with youth who are in conflict with the law, I have found that many of them struggle deeply with identity. Some do not know who they are, while others hide or suppress their true selves (especially when they have experienced rejection or shame for expressing who they were). This crisis of identity is often rooted in a pattern of instability and trauma that extends beyond the individual, and into family and community history.

Many of the young people involved in the juvenile justice system have experienced unstable family relationships, and have been exposed to unhealthy dynamics. In some cases, this is part of a generational cycle where parents or other family members were also involved with the system. In other cases, the youth may have been raised in estranged or non-nurturing environments, leading them to seek belonging in negative peer groups or harmful social circles.

Some of these youth have experienced significant trauma, including sexual violence and physical abuse. In the absence of a supportive family structure, many of them form strong bonds with peers who, despite being involved in negative behavior, offer a sense of belonging that feels more like family. In these groups, whether called gangs, teams, or something else, they find identity, support, and loyalty that they feel is missing elsewhere in their lives.

A common theme among these youth is a deep mistrust of systems and authority figures. They often view anyone associated with the justice or social services systems as adversaries. Unfortunately, this perception is sometimes reinforced by past experiences of discrimination, stigma, or being judged harshly by people in positions of power. It is also important to recognize that young people often generalize based on one negative experience. One harmful interaction with a youth worker, police officer, or probation officer can cause them to mistrust the entire system.

The truth is, many of these youths have never had the opportunity to form healthy, trusting, and non-judgmental relationships with adults, even within their own families. As the saying goes, "charity begins at home", yet many of them didn't experience compassion or support in their homes.

In this chapter, we will take an in-depth look at this subject of youth in conflict with the law, beginning with the biases these young people often face.

Bias, Stigma, And Youth In Conflict With The Law

When we examine the experiences of youth in conflict with the law, we quickly discover that their journeys are often shaped by layers of bias that compound their struggles and impede their healing. These biases create barriers that extend far beyond individual prejudices, becoming systemic obstacles that can determine a young person's entire life trajectory.

Let us consider a few of them.

Racial bias is one of the most common forms of biases suffered by youth in conflict with the law. In the United States, Black youth are five times more likely to be detained or committed than white youth, and Latino youth are 65% more likely to be detained (Sentencing Project, 2023). This happens even when the circumstances of their crimes are similar. This kind of bias can lead to an ongoing cycle where these youth are seen as "predisposed" to criminal behavior, which further perpetuates discrimination and reduces their chances of reintegration into society.

The next on the list is economic bias. Poverty often compounds the challenges faced by youth in conflict with the law. Kids from low-income neighborhoods may be more exposed to crime due to environmental factors like high crime rates, limited access to quality education, and a lack of social services.

These factors can lead to a stereotype that these youths are inherently involved in crime. The lack of access to resources also means they might not have the support systems or opportunities to avoid brushes with the law. This bias can lead to a vicious cycle where their economic circumstances lead to criminalization, which then further isolates them from opportunities to improve their situation.

When it comes to gender, male youth (especially those from marginalized backgrounds) often face harsher treatment. They are more likely to be incarcerated and receive longer sentences than their female counterparts for similar offenses. This is where we talk about gender bias.

However, gender bias can manifest in different ways depending on the offense. For instance, girls involved in sex-related offenses or running away from home might face stronger societal condemnation compared to boys. They are often perceived as more damaged or morally corrupt, which can compound their stigmatization.

Furthermore, male youth involved in similar offenses might be viewed as simply acting out, whereas girls may be portrayed as more manipulative or sexually deviant. Biases like these complicate the rehabilitation process, as they may lead to harsher punishments, reduced opportunities for reintegration, and a cycle of criminal behavior. Overcoming these biases requires systemic changes, and a deeper understanding of the underlying causes of youth crime

Personal, past, and unresolved trauma has been a long-standing reason why young people often get into trouble with the law. I know this because I have worked with a number of youths from diverse cultures, and helped them to heal. Let me share two stories. One is about a youth named Anthony (an Indigenous young person I worked with in both a foster group home and the community), and another about Keegan, a Western youth I also worked with.

From An Indigenous Perspective

(Anthony's Story)

When Anthony entered the system, he was isolated and struggled to build relationships. He had legal issues such as breaching curfew and was previously charged with theft and underage possession of drugs and alcohol.

His early life was marked by domestic violence, and he was apprehended at a young age. Young Anthony ended up living with extended family—his uncle and cousins—but as he would later share with us, these relationships felt more like obligations than connections. He described feeling like an outsider in his own family, tolerated rather than truly welcomed.

Though I wasn't directly assigned to Anthony, I observed his progress and interactions closely. One notable influence in his journey was his probation officer (PO), who stood out from others in the system. Unlike many POs who stick strictly to their job scope due to heavy caseloads, this PO went above and beyond. He built a genuine, trusting relationship with Anthony and made consistent efforts to check in with the youth workers and staff involved in Anthony's life. These efforts, though not formally required, made a significant impact. As Anthony felt more supported and understood, his behavior improved, and his willingness to engage with staff increased.

One reason this PO may have connected so well with Anthony was his cultural awareness. Although he was not Indigenous himself, he had taken time to learn about the culture, spoke a few words in the language, and had experience working with Indigenous youth. His ability to connect in a culturally informed and respectful way helped bridge the gap and made a meaningful difference in Anthony's journey.

This story highlights the power of relationships and cultural understanding in supporting youth in conflict with the law, especially Indigenous youth who often face layers of systemic disadvantage. Positive change happens when youth feel seen, heard, and respected. It reminds us that even small acts of genuine care can shift the trajectory of a young person's life.

Signs and Symptoms of Youth in Conflict with the Law
(in Anthony's Case)

Looking closely at Anthony's story, I can identify several key indicators that often signal that young people are struggling with legal issues, and the underlying trauma that frequently drives their behavior.

Social isolation and relationship difficulties are often the first signs I notice. These youths tend to withdraw from healthy connections while simultaneously testing boundaries with authority figures. Anthony's inability to build relationships and his strained family connections exemplify this pattern.

Escalating legal violations typically follow a progression from minor breaches to more serious charges. In Anthony's case, this started with curfew violations and progressed to theft and substance-related offenses. Additionally, cultural disconnection sometimes plays a significant role, particularly for Indigenous youth who may feel severed from their identity and community.

Anthony's Healing Journey

Anthony's healing journey demonstrates the transformative power of genuine relationship and cultural connection. His recovery began when he encountered a Probation Officer who refused to see him as just another case number. This PO understood that healing happens through relationships, not just through compliance with legal requirements.

The key elements of Anthony's healing included consistent, reliable adult support that went beyond professional obligations, cultural reconnection that enhanced communication with him, and gradual trust-building that allowed him to lower his defensive barriers.

His probation officer's cultural awareness and respect created a bridge between Anthony's past trauma and his potential future. As Anthony experienced genuine care and cultural validation, his willingness to engage increased, his behavior improved, and he began to envision possibilities for himself beyond the cycle of conflict he had known. This approach is crucial, especially when it has to do with indigenous youths.

Anthony's journey to healing teaches us that healing is possible when we approach youths with genuine respect, cultural awareness, and the understanding that their legal troubles are often symptoms of deeper pain that requires compassionate, informed intervention. This is particularly important for social workers, and personnel in correctional facilities.

From A Western Perspective

In recent years, professionals like psychologists, therapists, social workers, and other experts in the field have adapted various approaches to better support youth in the criminal justice system. One of these (Western) approaches is the trauma-informed approach, which focuses on understanding and addressing the trauma these youths have often experienced.

What is the Trauma-Informed Approach?

As discussed earlier in this book, the trauma-informed approach emphasizes the recognition of the impact of past trauma on a person's behavior and mental health. This approach shifts the perspective from asking *"What's wrong with you?"* to *"What happened to you?"* It involves understanding that the behaviors we see in youths in the system may be a direct result of unresolved trauma from their past.

For many youths, their issues with the law may be directly linked to experiences of violence, neglect, or strained relationships with their caregivers. Many of these young people may have been exposed to substance abuse, domestic violence, or abandonment, thereby creating complex layers of trauma.

In psychology, this is sometimes referred to as comorbid conditions—when two or more disorders exist simultaneously. This might mean that a youth who is in conflict with the law could also struggle with substance or alcohol addiction, mental health challenges (like anxiety and depression), or physical disabilities (such as hearing loss).

I once worked with a youth named Keegan at a group home specifically designed for youth in conflict with the law. Keegan was a very outgoing and respectful young man. He got along with his peers, followed the rules in the home, and had no history of violence within the group home environment. However, Keegan's history was far from peaceful.

(Keegan's Story)

Keegan had grown up in a violent household where he experienced physical abuse, and was exposed to drugs (specifically meth) at a very young age. The issue for Keegan was that, whenever he left the safety of the home and encountered drugs, he would act out violently. This behavior was very different from how he acted in the group home, where he was calm and respectful.

When Keegan became violent, he would assault others and sometimes break into properties, which led to legal trouble.

As I built a relationship with Keegan based on trust, he began to open up about his experiences. He shared that he often felt extreme anxiety, and sometimes even panic attacks, due to the violence he had witnessed in his childhood. Additionally, when law enforcement officers detained him, Keegan would feel as if he were being treated unfairly, as though he was "a piece of shit" and judged harshly by the authorities. This made it even harder for him to remain calm and in control.

Signs & Symptoms of Youth in Conflict with the Law
(in Keegan's Case)

From Keegan's story, several critical indicators can be identified, and these can help us understand the complex relationship between trauma, substance use, and legal troubles in young people. Environmental behavioral inconsistency is one of the most telling signs, and this shows up when youths who are calm and respectful in structured, safe environments become violent or aggressive when exposed to certain triggers or substances. This dramatic shift in behavior often indicates that their actions are more about trauma responses than intentional criminal behavior.

Substance-triggered violence represents another significant pattern, where specific drugs or substances act as catalysts for aggressive behavior. In Keegan's case, methamphetamine didn't just impair his judgment, but seemed to unlock years of stored trauma and rage. I have observed that youths exhibiting this pattern often have histories of early substance exposure, particularly in chaotic family environments where drugs were normalized or where they were used as coping mechanisms for abuse.

Trauma-based anxiety and panic responses frequently manifest as extreme anxiety, panic attacks, and hypervigilance that stem from childhood exposure to violence. These youth often describe feeling constantly on edge, being easily startled by sudden movements or loud noises, and experiencing physical symptoms like racing heartbeat, sweating, or difficulty breathing when triggered.

Authority-related re-traumatization is also common among youth from abusive backgrounds. These young people often experience interactions with law enforcement as extensions of the abuse they suffered at home. They may interpret normal police procedures as personal attacks, feel judged and devalued by authority figures, and respond with increased aggression or defiance when they perceive unfair treatment. This creates a cycle where their negative expectations of authority figures become self-fulfilling prophecies.

It is worth knowing that explosive, impulsive criminal behavior often differs from calculated criminal activity. These youths typically engage in property crimes, assault, or other offenses during moments of extreme emotional dysregulation rather than for financial gain or strategic purposes. The crimes often seem disproportionate to any logical motivation and are frequently committed under the influence of substances that lower inhibitions and heighten emotional responses.

Finally, we see how chronic feelings of worthlessness and shame present themselves when these youths interact with systems and authority figures. Youths like Keegan often internalize negative messages about their worth, believing they are bad or damaged individuals. This deep-seated shame affects how they interpret actions of people toward them, often assuming the worst intentions even from people trying to help them. Their self-concept becomes so negative that they expect rejection and harsh treatment, which can lead to defensive or aggressive responses even in neutral situations.

Keegan's Healing Journey (Trauma-Informed Support)

One of the key things I learned through working with Keegan was how important language and the way we relate to these youths really is. When we communicate with youths who have experienced significant trauma, we must be mindful of our words and actions. The language we use can either help build trust or perpetuate feelings of shame and judgment.

I worked closely with Keegan to develop a plan that made sense for him—one that would reduce his exposure to drugs, and in turn, reduce his risk of acting out violently. Together, we set up a schedule where he would stay home after school, participating in activities he enjoyed, such as playing games with the other residents at the group home.

At first, this structure was difficult for Keegan. He had been in several group homes before, but none had provided the kind of consistent structure that we were trying to implement. Over time, however, he began to embrace this new routine. It helped him feel safer and more in control, and it allowed him to focus on working through his probation orders without further misconduct.

When I last checked in with Keegan after he left the group home, I was happy to hear that he had graduated from high school, and had less probation orders or issues. He even occasionally returns to the group home to mentor other youths, showing that the right kind of support and structure can truly make a difference.

Sources Of Trauma for Youth In Conflict With The Law

For young people like Anthony and Keegan, the behaviors that eventually led to their involvement with the law were the direct result of years of personal trauma. Anthony had grown up in a household marked by neglect and abandonment, which left him feeling like he had no place in the world.

Keegan, on the other hand, came from an environment of physical abuse, where violence became not only a coping mechanism but also a way of gaining a sense of control. Neither of them had the tools or the support to understand the emotional pain they were carrying, so it manifested outwardly as anger, violence, and defiance.

The justice system itself can become another source of trauma for young people. Research by the American Psychological Association (2023) indicates that youth who experience incarceration show higher rates of depression, anxiety, and post-traumatic stress disorder compared to their peers. The loss of freedom, separation from family, and exposure to institutional violence can compound existing trauma, and create new wounds that further impede healing.

For Anthony, the process of arrest and detention reinforced his belief that he was unwanted and disposable. For Keegan, the harsh environment of juvenile detention initially triggered more violent responses, as it reminded him of the abusive home environment he had tried to escape.

Understanding these experiences is essential for any intervention to be effective. Trauma, especially when experienced in childhood, rewires the brain and influences behavior in profound ways. This is why youths like Anthony and Keegan may struggle to make rational decisions, seek out dangerous peer groups, or engage in self-destructive behaviors. It is not a matter of simply making "better choices" but understanding the emotional and psychological weight that is influencing their every action.

Healing Pathways For Youth In Conflict With The Law

(From An Afrocentric Perspective)

I have spent years studying youth justice systems around the world, and I can tell you that Africa's approach to helping young people in conflict with the law is refreshingly different from what you'll find anywhere else. Before we go into details, let me share some numbers that might be of interest to you.

Across Africa, young people under 25 make up over 60% of the population, which means we are talking about hundreds of millions of young lives. When these young people find themselves in trouble with the law, it's rarely just about individual bad choices. Research shows that youth crime is often a symptom of deeper community wounds like poverty, displacement, lack of opportunity, and disconnection from cultural roots (United Nations Office on Drugs and Crime, 2015).

Interestingly, African governments have responded to this reality. Countries like South Africa, Kenya, and Ghana have developed justice systems that blend traditional healing practices with modern legal frameworks, thereby creating something entirely new and remarkably effective. In regions where community-based interventions have been implemented, recidivism (the tendency of a convicted criminal to reoffend) rates among young offenders have dropped significantly compared to areas relying solely on detention (Institute for Security Studies, 2018). This success isn't accidental, but largely attributed to the

African philosophical principle of Ubuntu, which roughly translates to "I am because we are."

Now, let us reflect on this very remarkable healing program which took place in Sierra Leone.

After the devastating civil war in 2002, Sierra Leonean Non-Governmental Organizations (NGOs) introduced dance and movement therapy for former child soldiers. These were young people who had been forced to witness and participate in unimaginable violence, and traditional counseling approaches weren't working partly because sitting in a room talking about trauma felt foreign to many of these young survivors.

The local NGOs, working with international partners, tried something that might seem unusual but was actually deeply rooted in African culture. That was dance and movement therapy. I know what you might be thinking: "Dance therapy for traumatized child soldiers? Really?" But here's the thing. This approach recognizes that trauma doesn't just live in our minds, but in our bodies. Our muscles remember violence, our nervous systems stay on high alert, and sometimes our bodies hold memories that our minds can't process through words alone.

As these young people began to move, their bodies started to remember what it felt like to be human rather than juvenile soldiers with ammunition. Participants didn't just process their own trauma, they used their bodies to tell their stories, not just the stories of violence, but stories of who they were before the war and who they wanted to become.

The transformation that happened in these sessions was remarkable. Research documenting this approach found that dance interventions helped participants reconnect with their cultural identity while processing trauma in a way that felt natural and healing (Olsson, 2013). Former child soldiers began to discover that their bodies could create beauty instead of destruction, that their movements could generate healing rather than harm. The therapy sessions became a bridge between their traumatic past and their hopeful future, allowing them to integrate their experiences without being defined by them.

As a result of this practice, individual healing rippled outward into the community. The dance sessions evolved into communal performances where former child soldiers could share their healing journey with their families and neighbours. In Sierra Leonean culture, healing has always been understood as a community process, so when these young people performed their stories through dance, they were inviting their communities to witness their transformation and participate in their healing.

Moreso, participants began to see themselves not as former child soldiers, but as healers and peacemakers. The dance therapy sessions became a powerful example of how Afrocentric healing approaches can address even the most severe trauma by grounding therapeutic techniques in African cultural practices and worldviews.

Today, many of the former child soldiers who participated in these dance therapy programs have become community leaders, advocates, and healers in their own right. Their journey from trauma to healing to leadership speaks of the transformative power of culturally rooted approaches to youth rehabilitation. The Sierra Leone dance therapy model has inspired similar programs across Africa and beyond, and is a testament to the fact that healing approaches rooted in African traditional practices can be universally applicable.

(From A Faith-Based Perspective)

Faith practices across the globe are also very important in the healing process, as they provide youths with the framework for understanding forgiveness, redemption, and personal transformation. For many youths in conflict with the law, spiritual healing becomes an essential component of their recovery journey, offering hope and meaning that transcends their circumstances. So, while the methods and beliefs may differ, the core principles of forgiveness, redemption, and personal transformation are common threads in most faiths.

In Christianity, for example, healing is rooted in forgiveness and redemption. The Bible teaches that no one is beyond God's grace, and through repentance, individuals can experience spiritual renewal (1

John 1:9). The parable of the Prodigal Son (Luke 15:11-32) serves as a powerful example of unconditional love and second chances, illustrating that no matter how far someone has strayed, there is always a path back to wholeness.

For youths like Anthony who struggled with feelings of abandonment and worthlessness, Christian teachings about God's unconditional love provided a foundation for healing. The concept that he was "fearfully and wonderfully made" (Psalm 139:14) helped counteract the negative messages he had internalized about himself. Christian-based rehabilitation programs report a 60% reduction in recidivism rates compared to traditional secular programs (Prison Fellowship, 2023).

Hinduism offers a unique perspective on healing through the concepts of karma and dharma. While karma acknowledges that actions have consequences, it also emphasizes that individuals have the power to change their destiny through righteous action (dharma). This philosophy can be particularly healing for youth who feel trapped by their circumstances or past mistakes.

The Hindu concept of Atman (true self) teaches that beneath the pain and dysfunction lies an eternal, perfect essence that cannot be damaged by external circumstances. This understanding can provide profound comfort to youth who have experienced severe trauma, helping them recognize that their true identity transcends their experiences.

Similarly, in Islam, the concept of Tawbah (repentance) allows individuals to seek forgiveness from Allah, turning away from sin and making amends. This path of personal growth and renewal is also central to Hinduism, where the idea of karma encourages individuals to take responsibility for their actions, seek redemption, and realign with dharma (righteousness).

In Buddhism, healing comes through self-awareness and the Eightfold Path, which encourages moral conduct, meditation, and wisdom. The emphasis on letting go of attachments and finding inner peace mirrors the Christian pursuit of spiritual renewal and the Buddhist path of inner calm. The Buddhist emphasis on compassion—both for oneself and others—can be profoundly healing for youth who carry tremendous guilt and shame. Meditation practices taught in Buddhist tradition have been shown to reduce symptoms of PTSD and depression, making them valuable tools in the healing process (American Psychological Association, 2023).

Across all faith traditions, spiritual practices such as prayer and meditation provide powerful tools for healing. These practices offer youth ways to connect with something greater than themselves, find peace in the midst of chaos, and develop the inner resources necessary for transformation.

Prayer, whether in the Christian tradition of personal communion with God, the Islamic practice of Salat, or the Jewish tradition of structured liturgical prayer, provides a framework for processing emotions, seeking guidance, and finding hope. Research by the National Center for Health Statistics (2023) shows that youths who engage in regular prayer have lower rates of substance abuse and higher levels of emotional resilience.

Meditation practices, whether rooted in Buddhist mindfulness, Hindu yoga, or Christian contemplative traditions, offer youth tools for managing difficult emotions and developing self-awareness. These practices can be particularly beneficial for youths who have experienced trauma, as they provide ways to calm the nervous system and develop emotional regulation skills.

Pathways to Rehabilitation *(The Way Forward)*

Education is one of the most powerful tools in breaking the cycle of crime and rehabilitation. For youth like Anthony and Keegan, academic disengagement and a lack of employment opportunities were both contributors to their criminal behavior and significant barriers to their future success.

For Anthony, his troubles at school were not due to a lack of intelligence, but rather a lack of support. Without a stable home environment or a safe space to learn, he became disengaged, and his grades dropped. This disengagement led to feelings of failure, which in turn fueled his anger and frustration. The lack of academic success made him feel as though he had no future, which contributed to his later involvement with the law.

Keegan struggled with finding meaningful employment. With a criminal record and little job experience, he was often overlooked in the job market, leading him to feel like he was stuck in a cycle of poverty and crime. However, through targeted educational and vocational programs, both Anthony and Keegan found paths to personal growth. Vocational training provided them with practical skills that improved their employability, while educational programs offered a new perspective on their potential.

Creating opportunities for education and employment for youth in conflict with the law not only equips them with skills but also provides them with a sense of purpose and direction. This, in turn, reduces the likelihood of recidivism, as young people are less likely to reoffend when they see a positive future for themselves.

Mentorship also plays an important role in the rehabilitation process. Positive adult figures can offer the guidance and support that many of these youth never received at home or in their communities. Mentors help youth build trust in adults, develop coping strategies, and make healthier life choices.

For Anthony, his mentor had been through a similar circumstance. Through their relationship, Anthony learned that success wasn't about money or status, but about having a vision for the future and taking small, consistent steps to achieve it. His mentor encouraged him to explore career options, build his resume, and focus on his personal growth. With this guidance, Anthony began to take ownership of his life and his choices.

Keegan's mentor, on the other hand, had many of the same struggles Keegan had experienced. Their bond allowed Keegan to develop resilience and learn how to manage stress and frustration in healthier ways. By seeing his mentor's success story, Keegan started to believe that change was possible for him as well. Mentorship can also help provide emotional support during times of crisis, reminding youths that there are people who believe in their potential. The stability that mentors offer can be the cornerstone of a young person's recovery and reintegration into society.

Building restorative communities is another pathway to helping youths in conflict with the law to heal. A restorative community is about creating an environment where youth feel supported, valued, and capable of change. These communities are often made up of local organizations, community leaders, families, and peers who work together to support youth in conflict with the law.

Anthony and Keegan both benefited from the collective efforts of such communities. Anthony's community support system was centered around his probation officer, his mentor, and a youth program that offered both academic and emotional support. Through these relationships, Anthony slowly began to believe in himself and his ability to make a positive contribution to society.

Keegan's restorative community was shaped by his group home, where staff members, counselors, and fellow residents worked together to create a culture of accountability and healing. It was here that Keegan learned to express himself in healthier ways, engage in activities that promoted emotional regulation, and build bonds with others who understood his struggles. The sense of belonging that came from being part of a supportive, non-judgmental group was transformative.

Restorative communities make it clear to youth that they are not alone in their struggles. These communities offer a network of care, where youth are encouraged to be vulnerable, seek support when needed, and ultimately find healing together. It is through these collective efforts that youths like Anthony and Keegan are able to rise above their pasts, and move toward brighter futures.

While individual interventions are critical, lasting change also requires systemic transformation. Our current justice system often prioritizes punitive measures over rehabilitative ones. If we truly want to support youth in conflict with the law, we must advocate for policies that focus on rehabilitation, healing, and reintegration rather than punishment.

This means pushing for legislation that promotes restorative justice practices, funding for trauma-informed programs, and the creation of rehabilitation centers that offer educational and vocational training. Additionally, policies that remove barriers to employment for formerly incarcerated youths, such as expunging criminal records for young offenders, are essential for breaking the cycle of poverty and crime.

Speaking of restorative justice practices, I would like us to zone in on how this plays out in Nigeria, a multi-ethnic West-African nation with a population of over 227 million people (according to Worldometer, and as at July 2025). The youth population in Nigeria currently stands at 160 million, little wonder why Nigeria is regarded as a country of the young by UNICEF.

Restorative Justice Practices *(From A Nigerian Perspective)*

Nigeria has a rich and vast cultural heritage, and this vastness does not exclude traditional justice systems that embody restorative principles for contemporary youth justice approaches. Traditional justice in Nigeria does not necessarily encourage the apportioning of blame, or having a winner and a loser. These systems, which predate colonial influences, prioritize healing, restoration, and community harmony over punishment and retribution.

The Igbo customary law system for instance, exemplifies restorative principles through its emphasis on *omenaala* (tradition) and community resolution of conflicts. In traditional Igbo society, when a young person engaged in harmful behavior, the extended family *(umunna)* and community elders would gather to understand the root causes and develop collective solutions. This process focuses on restoring balance within the community, rather than punishing the individual. The young person would be guided through rituals of acknowledgment, making amends, and reintegration into the community.

For the Yorubas, the *Agbegbe* system leverages community assemblies where conflicts are resolved through dialogue, mediation, and consensus-building. Elders, family members, and community representatives gather to hear all sides of a dispute and work toward solutions that address underlying issues while maintaining community harmony. For young people, this process includes guidance from elders who share wisdom about proper behavior while acknowledging the challenges of growing up. The emphasis is on teaching and learning rather than punishment, with the understanding that young people need support and guidance to develop into responsible adults.

In northern Nigeria, traditional Islamic justice systems incorporate concepts of *islah* (reform) and *tawbah* (repentance) that emphasize healing and transformation over punishment. Islamic mediation processes bring together religious leaders, family members, and community representatives to address conflicts through dialogue and mutual understanding. Young people are encouraged to acknowledge their mistakes, seek forgiveness, and demonstrate their commitment to change through positive actions. The community, in turn, provides support and opportunities for the young person to rebuild their reputation and relationships.

The Hausa-Fulani mediation system emphasizes reconciliation through *sulhu* (peaceful settlement) processes that prioritize relationship repair over punishment. When conflicts arise, respected community members facilitate discussions between affected parties to understand root causes and develop mutually acceptable solutions. For the youths, this process includes guidance from elders and opportunities to make amends through community service or other restorative actions. The approach is based on the understanding that young people are still developing, and need support rather than rejection when they make mistakes.

In Efik and Ibibio cultures, long before current systems like Alternative Dispute Resolution came in, these communities had their own ways of resolving conflict, especially when it involved the young. A person who wronged the community wasn't just judged based on what they did, but also based on who they were, what led them there, and how they could make things right.

The elders (often referred to as *Obong* for a singular person, and *mbong* for a collection of elders) would sit in a circle, listen, ask questions, hear from all sides, and most importantly, invite the offender to speak.

Offenders, especially the young ones, were often made to confess openly—not just to the elders, but to the people they hurt. In many cases, restitution followed: sometimes through labor, gifts, or symbolic acts that restored dignity to the victim and peace to the parties involved.

Another aspect of rehabilitation which must not be overlooked, is helping and empowering youth in conflict with the law to learn to advocate for themselves. For many of these youth, a lack of agency and control over their lives is a key factor that leads them down a destructive path. They feel powerless to change their circumstances, and this sense of helplessness can fuel their involvement in criminal behavior. Learning self-advocacy empowers youth like Anthony and Keegan to take control of their lives and future. This might mean advocating for their own mental health care, standing up for their right to education or employment, or even negotiating better relationships with their families.

Keegan, for instance, became an advocate for youth in his community, sharing his story and speaking out against the stigma that people with criminal backgrounds face. His ability to advocate for himself and others gave him a renewed sense of purpose and autonomy. Similarly, Anthony, once disengaged and cynical, began using his voice to help others in similar situations. Self-advocacy doesn't just improve individual outcomes; it contributes to the greater good by empowering youth to act as change agents in their own lives and communities. This shift from victimhood to empowerment is crucial for long-term transformation.

Now, how often do we pause to dig beyond the surface when dealing with these youths? In my years of working with young people involved with the criminal justice system, I can say that many of them face underlying mental health issues and substance abuse problems. These dual diagnoses complicate their ability to function in society and often contribute to their criminal behavior.

For Anthony, substance abuse was an issue that had been a constant throughout his life. He turned to drugs and alcohol as a way to cope with the trauma of his childhood. However, through counseling and support groups, he began to confront these issues and work through his addiction. This wasn't a quick or easy process, but with the right support, Anthony was able to begin his recovery journey.

Keegan had similar struggles, but his substance abuse was more closely linked to his emotional trauma. He had turned to drugs as a means to numb the pain of his past abuse. Addressing his mental health through therapy, peer support, and alternative coping strategies helped Keegan not only overcome his substance use, but also better understand the emotions that had driven his actions. Providing access to mental health care and substance abuse treatment is crucial for breaking the cycle of crime. These services must be integrated into the rehabilitation process to ensure that youth are receiving comprehensive support.

Summarily, the rehabilitation of youth in conflict with the law must be a holistic and multifaceted process, and this requires a comprehensive approach that takes into account not only the legal and social aspects but also the psychological, emotional, cultural, and physical dimensions of the individual.

Youth like Anthony and Keegan benefit from an approach that integrates therapy, family support, education, employment, mentorship, and community engagement. Each of these components plays a vital role in creating an environment where the youth can truly heal and grow. This holistic approach does more than reduce recidivism. Rather, it fosters the development of resilient, empowered individuals who can contribute positively to their communities.

For Anthony and Keegan, the journey was long, but it was also transformative. It wasn't a matter of simply staying out of trouble, but creating new pathways for their futures, regaining their sense of self-worth, and finding their place in the world. By embracing a holistic approach, we open the door for these youth to rewrite their stories and become agents of change in their own lives and beyond.

The Ripple Effect
(How Rehabilitated Youth Impact Society)

As we reflect on the journeys of Anthony, Keegan, The former child soldiers of Sierra Leone and countless other youth in conflict with the law, it is clear that their rehabilitation does more than just change their individual trajectories. It sparks a ripple effect that extends beyond their own lives to positively impact their families, communities, and society at large. When these young people are given the opportunity to heal, grow, and find their purpose, they become powerful agents of change who break the cycles of crime and trauma that once defined their existence.

The signs and symptoms these young people exhibited (behavioral volatility, substance use as self-medication, feelings of social exclusion, and conflicts with authority) were not random acts of rebellion but predictable responses to trauma, poverty, and disconnection. What their healing journeys teach us is that small changes, like providing structure in a young person's life, can have a profound impact.

Establishing routines and consistent expectations gives youth in the system the opportunity to develop healthier patterns. They begin to see that their actions have consequences, but that those consequences can be managed with the right support. The key insight from all three stories is that healing happens where there is a strong relationship hinged on trust.

When these youth are able to reintegrate into society with dignity, they inspire others to make better choices and rise above their circumstances. They become examples of resilience, showing that change is possible, no matter how difficult the journey. Their success stories, fueled by empathy, mentorship, cultural reconnection, and trauma-informed care, serve as beacons of hope for others still caught in the destructive cycles of crime and trauma.

Moreover, the work done to heal these youth does not just change them. It also changes the systems that allowed them to fall through the cracks in the first place. By addressing the root causes of their behavior and providing them with the tools for healing, we create a society that is more compassionate, more just, and more committed to offering second chances.

For parents, caregivers, and social workers, these stories offer crucial lessons about the power of seeing beyond behavior to the person underneath. Building positive, trusting relationships with these youth is crucial. When they feel heard, understood, and respected, they are more likely to open up and engage in the process of change.

This is why it is so important to focus on trauma-informed practices, and to approach these young people not just as offenders, but as individuals with complex histories that need healing and support.

CHAPTER FIVE
HEALING FOR CHILDREN & YOUTH WITH ALCOHOL OR DRUG CODEPENDENCY

"Young people healing from drug and alcohol dependence is a slow and quiet journey. Some days there's movement, and other days there isn't. But patience and persistence are the key to helping youth stay grounded while supporting them." - Eseosa Omoregie

Before I tell you about Jane, I want you to understand a few things.

When we talk about youth struggling with substance use, we're not just talking about addiction to drugs. We are talking about pain. Substance dependence means a youth's body and mind has adapted to drugs or alcohol to the point where stopping feels impossible. And the deeper issue often isn't the substance, but what they are using it to escape from.

Statistics from the World Health Organization Regional Office for Europe reveal that roughly 1 in 10 (9%) adolescents across all age groups have experienced significant drunkenness (being drunk at least twice) in their lifetime, a rate that alarmingly climbs from 5% at age 13 to 20% by age 15. In the United States alone, 407,000 teenagers aged 12 to 17-years-old met the criteria for Alcohol Use Disorder (AUD) in the last year. These numbers represent young lives caught in cycles of suffering that require our deepest understanding and most sustainable approaches to healing.

Regional differences tell us even more about the complexity of this crisis. Youths living in Western states and New England are the most likely to have abused drugs in the last four weeks, while urban centers often present different challenges and opportunities than rural communities. This variation underscores why we need healing approaches that are not one-size-fits-all, but rather flexible, culturally responsive, and deeply rooted in understanding each young person's unique context.

Many of the youth I've worked with are survivors of trauma, loss, or instability. Others are caught in cycles of grief they were never taught to understand, let alone process. For these youths, using drugs can feel like the only way to stay alive. And this is where harm reduction comes in.

Harm reduction does not mean encouraging drug use, it only means creating an atmosphere for safety, even when someone isn't ready to stop. It means meeting them where they are, not where we think they should be. And trauma-informed care? It simply means approaching these young people with compassion, knowing that their behaviors are often rooted in pain we cannot always see.

(Jane's Story)

Jane was one of those kids whose pain was easy to judge from the outside. Fifteen, charged with theft, caught drinking underage, out of school, in and out of shelters, and nearly invisible to the system. She had been removed from her home after years of witnessing violence. Her parents separated, and neither remained actively in her life. Her aunt who was her only approved family contact was cold and strict. Jane once said, "She's just like the people who gave up on me before." She didn't feel safe anywhere, so she made her own world, one made of blurry nights, streetlights, and silence.

She was half Indigenous, and I want to mention something important about her context. She lived in a city in the western prairie region. I honestly believe that if she had been living in a more remote or northern area, it would have either reduced her access to substances or caused her substance misuse to manifest in a different way. In the prairie region where I worked, and particularly in the city, we had a higher concentration of Indigenous people, which meant Jane had more access to cultural network resources and connection to support.

Jane wasn't deeply connected to her cultural spirituality and didn't believe strongly in traditional practices. However, she loved certain activities that included beading and artsy dressmaking. She had more faith in her Christian beliefs, though she was Indigenous. She did not see herself as a practicing Christian, but did believe in her faith. She sometimes requested to be taken to, or visit a church, but she eventually stopped going due to her interaction with another teen and how she felt judged (or isolated) there. Jane loved the ambiance and memories of being present in church as a child, and often reminisced on the times her parents took her there every Sunday.

One thing I admired about Jane was that she always showed up to our sessions, even if late or high. That mattered.

We didn't start with "Let's fix you." We started with a juice box, a beanbag chair, and an unspoken agreement that I wouldn't push. At first, I didn't talk about quitting. I talked about her—who she was outside of the system, and weeks later, she opened up.

"I couldn't stop the pain of being separated from my parents..." she said one day. *"Even with the violence, they were still my family. I thought using drugs meant I had healed. But the more I did it, the more I felt like... this is who I am now. Like I couldn't come back."*

Her voice cracked on that last part. I didn't interrupt. I knew what she meant.

Progress was not linear. Some months, she showed real change. Other months, we were back at zero. But she kept returning. And that's what recovery often looks like—showing up again, even when it hurts.

"Sometimes you have the strength to stop..." she told me another time. *"But sometimes... your body's gotten used to it. You're not in control anymore. And the more you go into it, the more it feels like there's no coming back."*

She wasn't wrong. Dependence is both mental and physical. And when stopping too fast can cause more harm than good, the only way forward is steady and supported.

Today, Jane's story isn't over. She's still figuring it out. Because the truth is, healing doesn't always roar. Sometimes it whispers, "You're not alone," and that's enough to keep going.

Signs and Symptoms of Alcohol and Drug Dependency
(in Jane's Story)

From Jane's story, we can observe a number of signs that indicate when a young person is struggling with substance dependency. These signs often interweave with trauma responses, making it important for social workers to understand the full picture rather than focusing solely on the substance use itself. They include:

Physical and Behavioral Signs:

- Chronic lateness or inconsistent attendance (Jane was often late to sessions)
- Legal troubles related to substance use (Jane's underage drinking charges)
- Instability in living situations (Jane's experience in and out of shelters)
- Academic disruption (Jane being out of school)
- Physical dependence where the body has adapted to the substance

Emotional and Psychological Indicators:

- Using substances to cope with emotional pain ("I couldn't stop the pain of being separated from my parents")
- Feelings of lost identity tied to substance use ("this is who I am now")
- Sense of hopelessness about recovery ("Like I couldn't come back")
- Disconnection from support systems and cultural or spiritual practices
- Trauma responses manifesting through substance use

Social and Relational Signs:

- Isolation from family and supportive adults
- Difficulty maintaining relationships
- Engagement in risky behaviors to obtain substances
- Creating alternative social networks centered around substance use

- Feeling judged or rejected by traditional support systems

Systemic Indicators:

- Involvement with child welfare systems
- Multiple placement disruptions
- Lack of stable adult relationships
- Limited access to appropriate cultural or spiritual support

Jane's Healing Journey

With Jane, I developed and followed a model I have now come to believe in. I named it the RESTARP model, and it worked perfectly with Jane. The progression of this model began with building relationship first, then setting structure and goals, tracking progress, allowing autonomy, reinforcing effort, and always practicing patience.

The healing journey doesn't begin with treatment plans or interventions. It begins with connection. Jane showed up to our sessions, even when she was high, even when she was late. That consistency, that thread of connection, became the foundation everything else was built on.

We built monthly vision boards together: "Go to sleep before 2 AM." "Have one sober day this week." "Message a support person when tempted." These were small goals, but they were hers. That made them powerful.

We used harm reduction strategies too. She had safe words she could text me if she found herself in danger. She didn't always use them. But the fact that she could? That mattered. It gave her a sliver of power in a world that had taken so much of it.

The RESTARP Model

The RESTARP Model provides a roadmap for healing that is both structured and flexible, meeting youths where they are while gently guiding them toward their own definitions of recovery.

RE - Relationship First

Everything begins with relationship. Before we can talk about goals, progress, or healing, we must first establish genuine human connection. With Jane, this meant juice boxes and beanbag chairs. It meant showing up consistently, even when she didn't. It meant not leading with *"Let's fix you"* but rather with *"I see you, and you matter."*

Relationship-first means:
- Prioritizing connection over correction
- Meeting youth where they are, not where we think they should be
- Building trust through consistency and non-judgment
- Recognizing that the therapeutic relationship itself is healing
- Understanding that for many youths, we may be the first stable adult relationship they've experienced

S - Setting Structure and Goals

Once a relationship is established, we can begin to collaboratively create structure. This isn't about imposing external goals, but rather about helping youths identify their own aspirations and breaking them down into manageable steps. Jane's monthly vision boards were her goals, not mine. This ownership was crucial to their success.

Setting structure involves:
- Collaborative goal-setting that honors youth voice and choice
- Creating predictable routines and boundaries that feel safe
- Breaking large goals into smaller, achievable steps
- Establishing clear expectations while maintaining flexibility
- Building in regular check-ins and adjustments

T - Tracking Progress

Progress in healing from substance dependency is rarely linear. With Jane, some months brought real change, while others felt like starting over. Tracking progress means celebrating small victories, learning from setbacks, and maintaining hope even when forward movement

isn't visible.
Tracking includes:

- Documenting both quantitative and qualitative changes
- Celebrating small wins and incremental progress
- Analyzing patterns in both struggles and successes
- Adjusting approaches based on what's working and what isn't
- Maintaining long-term perspective on the healing journey

A - Allowing Autonomy

Perhaps the most challenging aspect of supporting youth with substance dependency is learning when to step back and allow them to make their own choices, even when those choices involve risk. Jane's safe words were available to her, but she didn't always use them. Respecting her autonomy meant accepting that the power to heal ultimately rested with her.

Allowing autonomy means:
- Respecting youth's right to make their own choices
- Providing information and support without coercion
- Balancing safety concerns with respect for self-determination
- Recognizing that control over one's own life is often what youth are seeking through substance use
- Trusting in young people's innate capacity for healing and growth

R - Reinforcing Effort

Recovery is about effort, not just outcomes. When Jane showed up late or high, I reinforced her effort to show up at all. When she managed one sober day instead of seven, we celebrated that one day. Reinforcing effort means recognizing that the journey itself is the destination.

Reinforcing effort includes:
- Acknowledging attempts, even when they don't lead to success
- Focusing on process rather than just outcomes
- Celebrating small steps and partial successes
- Providing positive reinforcement for healthy choices
- Building self-efficacy through recognition of personal strengths

P - Practicing Patience

Healing from substance dependency is a slow process that unfolds in its own time. There are no shortcuts, no quick fixes, and no guarantee of linear progress. Practicing patience means accepting that healing happens on the youth's timeline, not ours.

Practicing patience involves:
- Accepting that healing is a non-linear process
- Maintaining hope and commitment even during setbacks
- Resisting the urge to rush or force progress
- Understanding that relapse is often part of recovery
- Trusting in the long-term nature of healing and growth

I believe the RESTARP approach to healing is particularly important, given the global scope of youth substance dependency.

When we consider that millions of young people worldwide are struggling with these issues, it becomes clear that we need healing approaches that are not only effective but also sustainable and scalable. The RESTARP Model provides a framework that can be adapted to different cultural contexts, resource levels, and individual needs while maintaining its core principles of relationship, respect, and patience.

Factors Contributing To Alcohol Or Substance Use

I have always wanted to understand why young people indulge in alcohol and substance use the way they do. Not just that, I was curious to know what factors led to that behavior, and how they eventually got themselves hooked to a point where they could not return. So, I went deep into research, and from my findings, this unhealthy affinity with alcohol and drugs is not usually a one-way traffic.

What that means is that substance use and dependency does not happen as a result of one single factor. Several risk factors contribute to substance use among young people, and these include socio-economic factors such as poverty, unemployment, and lack of education. Social and environmental influences like peer pressure, family dynamics, and the availability of substances are also among them.

In sub-Saharan Africa, for instance, I have learned that young people often turn to substances as a way to cope with economic hardship, and pretty much escape from the realities of their existence.

The family where these youths come from also play a huge role, but it is not always in the ways we expect. It is not always a case of having bad parents or coming from a broken home. Sometimes, it's about families that are physically present but emotionally absent, or families that are so overwhelmed by their own struggles that they can't provide the support their children need. I must add that substance use by parents does not just model the behavior of their youth, but changes the family environment in ways that make substances more accessible, and normalize their use.

Also, youth with records of interpersonal violence, and youths who have experienced multiple past traumas or poly-victimization, are at the highest risk of developing these co-occurring disorders. This connection between trauma and substance use creates a vicious cycle that is particularly prevalent in regions affected by conflict, poverty, or social instability.

Another reason why many youths indulge in alcohol and substance use is peer pressure. In many Asian cultures, for example, the pressure to succeed academically is so intense that some young people turn to stimulants to maintain performance, or to depressants to cope with the stress. The peer pressure here isn't necessarily borne out of the need to just use substances, but to achieve impossible standards, and substances become the tool to bridge that gap.

I also hold the view that with regards to this generation, technology and social media are redefining the boundaries of substance use. While I couldn't find specific statistics in my research, what I am seeing globally is that social media creates new forms of peer pressure and comparison that previous generations never had to deal with. Young people in developed countries are constantly exposed to curated images of party culture, making substance use seem more glamorous and widespread than it actually is. Meanwhile, in developing regions, social media exposure to Western lifestyle trends can create desires for experiences that aren't appropriate.

The economic factor contributing to this is huge, but it works in two directions. In regions with high poverty, substances might be used as an escape from harsh realities, but they're also sometimes seen as a way to participate in an economy when legitimate opportunities are scarce. On the flip side, in wealthier regions, economic privilege can actually increase access to substances and create environments where expensive habits can be sustained longer before consequences become apparent.

There is also a strong connection between mental health and substance abuse, and this, we cannot ignore. Yes, substances could cause mental health problems, but that is not the point here. Young people often turn to substances to self-medicate for mental health issues that aren't being addressed properly, and this calls for concern. In many parts of the world, mental health services for young people are either non-existent or heavily stigmatized, thereby making substance use seem like the only available option for dealing with anxiety, depression, or trauma.

The final but very crucial factor here is availability, and this has to be the father of them all because what is not available cannot be used, not to mention being misused. The availability of substances in different regions of the world will definitely impact usage patterns. In some parts of the world, traditional substances like khat in East Africa or betel nuts in Southeast Asia are culturally embedded and easily accessible. In others, prescription medications diverted from legitimate medical use to become the substances of choice.

Essentially, as long as there is an ongoing globalization of drug markets, substances that were once regional problems will continue to spread worldwide, and this will undoubtedly create new challenges for prevention and treatment.

Now that we have uncovered crucial factors that pull young people into alcohol and drug dependency, let me take you through the Western and Afrocentric healing side of things. Thereafter, we will consider a number of systems that could promote healing, and also look at some unconventional approaches to helping youths heal from alcohol and substance dependency.

Western View On Healing

Like I mentioned earlier in this book, the foundation of Western recovery practices rests on evidence-based treatments. Such treatments, in this context, include Cognitive Behavioral Therapy (CBT), where young people learn to identify and change thought patterns that lead to substance use, and Motivational Interviewing, which doesn't tell the youth what to do, but helps them discover their own reasons for a change. These approaches work because they respect the autonomy of young people, while providing them with concrete tools for transformation.

It is no longer news that Western healing has started embracing what Indigenous cultures have known for centuries. Integrative recovery programs include sweat ceremonies, talking circles, prayers, smudging, and sessions with recognized spiritual healers and are combined with Western mainstream practices, such as group therapy and Alcoholics Anonymous meetings. Interesting, isn't it?

Let me share Jake's story, a nineteen year old Western youth who battled methamphetamine addiction for three years.

(Jake's Story)

What inspires me the most about Jake's journey wasn't just that he got clean, but how he did it.

His recovery began in a traditional residential program where he learned coping skills and went through detox, but I would say that real healing came when he started participating in adventure therapy like rock climbing, wilderness expeditions, and group challenges that rebuilt his confidence and showed him he could experience natural highs.

After one of his recovery expeditions, Jake had this to say about his experience: *"When I was standing on that cliff face, 200 feet up, completely sober and feeling more alive than I ever did on drugs, I realized I had been searching for that feeling in all the wrong places."*

For Jake, this turned out to be the best replacement for three whole years of addiction to drugs. What also worked in Jake's case were the Motivational Interviewing sessions he participated in. Obviously, there was a feeling that only the dependence on methamphetamine could give, but having discovered other hobbies that provided the same feeling and were not destructive, Jake saw reasons to gradually and completely abandon his former lifestyle of substance use.

Today, Jake works as a peer recovery coach and has been clean for four years. His story and healing journey is proof that healing from substance use is possible, and can be unlocked when youths are exposed to higher and better experiences.

Afrocentric View On Healing

Adunni, 22, struggled with alcohol dependency for two years after losing her father in a car accident. Her family explored different avenues like rehabilitation centers, counseling, even trying to send her abroad for treatment, yet nothing worked until her grandmother brought in a traditional healer.

The healing process began with divination. The healer sought to understand not just Adunni's drinking habit, but the spiritual and ancestral influences affecting her family line. They discovered that her father's sudden death had created what the healer called a "spiritual wound" that was affecting multiple family members in different ways.

The treatment involved several components that might seem foreign to Western eyes but made perfect sense within Adunni's cultural framework. First came the cleansing ceremonies. These were rituals that used specific herbs, prayers, and symbolic actions to "wash away" the spiritual contamination that was contributing to her addiction. The herbal components were sophisticated too. The healer prescribed specific plants that had been used for generations to help people overcome known addictions, some were used to cleanse the body, others to strengthen mental clarity, and still others to provide spiritual protection during the vulnerable recovery period.

The part that excites me about Adunni's recovery was how it addressed her grief, which had been the root cause of her drinking. Through ancestral communion practices, she was able to maintain connection with her father's spirit in healthy ways, rather than numbing the pain with alcohol.

Thankfully, her uncles, aunts, cousins, even family friends were involved in creating that atmosphere of support and accountability. Two years later, Adunni not only remains sober but has become a bridge (in her community) between traditional and modern healing approaches.

In Nigeria specifically, there are traditional practices called *"Egúngún"* ceremonies in Yoruba culture. Here, community members create sacred spaces for healing and transformation, and these ceremonies often involve drumming, dancing, and spiritual possession that allows for deep emotional release and community support. For young people struggling with addiction, participating in these ceremonies can provide powerful experiences of belonging and spiritual cleansing that complement or sometimes replace conventional treatment.

Another powerful Nigerian practice is the use of *"àgbo"* (traditional herbal preparations that are specifically designed to help with dependency issues). Unlike Western medications that often treat symptoms, these herbal combinations are believed to address the spiritual and energetic imbalances that contribute to addictive behaviors.

The Igbo culture has *"Ndi Dibia"*, a collection of traditional healers who specialize in understanding how spiritual and emotional disturbances manifest as physical and behavioral problems, including addiction. Their approach involves extensive consultation with the young person's entire family system, identifying patterns that may have contributed to the addiction, and prescribing not just herbs but specific rituals and lifestyle changes for the entire family.

Healing from alcohol and substance use, from an Afrocentric view, may involve practices that are not common, scientifically proven, or universally accepted. However, the strength of its effectiveness lies in its unique cultural and spiritual approaches. These can be leveraged, or combined with Indigenous or Western ways of healing.

Unconventional Paths To Healing

In addition to the healing approaches discussed above, here are a few (somewhat) unconventional ways to help youths heal from alcohol and substance abuse. These unconventional approaches aren't necessarily better or worse than traditional or clinical methods. They are different, and for some young people, they're exactly what works.

The first is adventure-based recovery, which is a fast-growing movement. This includes programs that take young people into nature, teach them to surf, climb mountains, or care for horses. These experiences work because they provide natural dopamine releases, build confidence, and create powerful metaphors for overcoming challenges. When you've just rappelled down a 100-foot cliff face while sober, facing your addiction suddenly seems more manageable.

Peer recovery programs are also revolutionizing treatment by putting young people who've been through addiction at the center of the healing process. The mission here is to provide life skills and peer support to help young people recover from substance use disorder, and ultimately reach their full potential. These programs work because they eliminate the power dynamic between the expert and the patient, instead, healing happens through authentic connection with people who truly understand the struggle.

Another unconventional approach gaining traction is micro-dosing mindfulness (not what you might think). This involves breaking down meditation and mindfulness practices into tiny, manageable pieces that fit into a young person's daily life. Instead of demanding an hour of meditation, it might be 30 seconds of conscious breathing before opening TikTok. Small steps, but they build neural pathways that support recovery.

Community service recovery programs are also showing incredible results in this aspect. Young people in recovery rebuild their sense of worth by contributing to their communities. They do this by teaching kids, cleaning up neighborhoods, or mentoring other struggling youths. This approach works because it transforms shame into purpose, and isolation into connection.

Finally, digital detox programs have emerged as powerful tools for healing, especially for young people whose substance use is intertwined with social media addiction or online escapism. These programs teach healthy relationships with technology while addressing underlying emotional needs that both substances and excessive screen time were trying to meet.

Healing Systems For Youths With Alcohol And Substance Use

Sustainable recovery for young people often requires multiple support systems working in harmony. Let's consider a number of them and how they can uniquely contribute to healing when they're operating at their best, starting with the legal system.

I know we had talked about this in the previous chapter, but I must reiterate that the most progressive developments I've seen in legal approaches involve shifting from punitive to restorative justice models specifically designed for young people. Drug courts for youth should now focus on treatment and community service rather than incarceration. Legal systems should begin to realize that criminalizing addiction often drives young people further underground, and away from help.

We should begin to see the emergence of more peer jury programs, where young people who have successfully overcome addiction help determine consequences and support plans for those just entering the system. This approach will be effective, as it will create authentic accountability between peers who truly understand each other's struggles.

Second to legal systems, are faith-based systems. I like the fact that religious communities are increasingly recognizing that shame and judgment push struggling youth away, rather than drawing them toward healing. The most effective faith-based recovery approaches I've encountered focus on unconditional love, community support, and practical assistance rather than moral lectures.

What I find remarkable about faith-based approaches to healing is its ability to address the spiritual emptiness that often underlies addiction. Many young people turn to substances because they're seeking transcendence, connection to something greater, or relief from existential pain. When religious communities provide healthy pathways to spiritual experiences through meditation, service, music, or contemplative practices, they are indirectly offering alternatives that meet the same deep needs that substances were attempting to fill.

From my experience, some Christian youths who believe in the Christian doctrine respond better to treatment. Over time, Christian recovery programs have incorporated elements like prayers, repentance from sinful practices, symposiums, seminars, and healing services that help young people experience God's presence in tangible ways. They also help the youth understand that their bodies are the temple of God, and as such, they cannot afford to live carelessly through reckless drinking and substance use. On the other hand, Islamic approaches emphasize the healing power of community prayer, the discipline of fasting, and the support of the *ummah* (community) in maintaining sobriety.

Clinical care models for struggling youths are not left out here. From my research, the most effective clinical approaches now integrate trauma therapy, family systems work, and peer support with medication-assisted treatment when appropriate. Personalized medicine approaches are beginning to consider genetic factors, cultural backgrounds, trauma histories, and individual preferences when designing treatment plans, and this should be scaled across regions of the world.

Lastly, no system is more crucial, or more complex, than family. Effective family involvement goes beyond simply getting parents to stop enabling or start setting boundaries. It involves helping entire family systems understand their roles in both the development and the healing of addiction in youths. Families must create environments that support recovery while maintaining healthy boundaries. This might involve parents learning new communication skills, siblings understanding their own trauma responses, or grandparents adapting cultural expectations to support rather than shame their recovering family member.

The key lesson from studying all of these approaches is that healing happens at the intersection of these approaches. It is not safe to say that one is better than the other, because no two youths or situations are the same. Young people who achieve lasting recovery are those who were treated with a combination of approaches that speaks to their unique needs, cultural background, and personal journey while being surrounded by systems that support rather than undermine their healing process.

Reflections And Conclusion

Before we conclude, I must stress that the path ahead (as far as healing is concerned) requires us to create more sustainable recovery support systems for our youths, while scaling available options that have proven to be effective. We must also resist the pressure for quick fixes, understanding that recovery is often measured in small victories. This includes showing up to a session, choosing one sober day, and reaching out for support instead of using substances to cope.

Our role as parents and social workers is not to force healing but create conditions where it becomes possible through safe relationships, responsive systems, culturally appropriate interventions, and communities that see potential rather than just problems. When we approach struggling youth with the understanding that their substance use represents pain seeking relief, we can meet them with the compassion, patience, and comprehensive support they need to find healthier ways to heal, connect, and thrive.

If you are a young person struggling with alcohol or substance use, I need you to know this: what you're going through isn't necessarily a moral flop or character flaw. It is basically pain seeking relief, and that pain is valid even if the way you're trying to manage it isn't working.

I know substances might feel like the only thing that helps right now, like the only way to make the hurt bearable, but I promise you there are other paths to healing that would not leave you feeling more trapped and hopeless. Start small. You don't have to quit everything tomorrow or have your whole life figured out. Maybe today it's reaching out to one trusted person, attending one support meeting, or trying one healthy activity that makes you feel alive.

Find your people, whether that's in a support group, through adventure therapy, in your faith community, or with a counselor who truly understands your journey. Remember that setbacks aren't failures but a part of the journey, and every time you choose to try again, you're proving your own strength.

Your story isn't over, your pain can become wisdom, and the very experiences that feel like they're destroying you can become the foundation for helping others heal. You're worth fighting for, your life has meaning beyond your current struggle, and recovery is absolutely possible for you.

CHAPTER SIX
HEALING FOR CHILDREN & YOUTH WITH ESTRANGED PARENT/GUARDIAN RELATIONSHIPS

What comes to your mind when you hear the word estranged?

For many, it's the image of broken relationships—an absence where there was once closeness, the slow drift of distance between parent and child. But for children, especially, estrangement is often far more profound. It is a rupture that cracks the very foundation of their emotional world. Children are still in the process of discovering who they are, and when a parent or guardian is no longer emotionally available, it feels as if the ground beneath them is shifting, threatening to swallow them whole.

Research tells us that a child's brain continues to develop until their mid-20s (ScienceDirect, 2010). This means that their formative years, when they're trying to understand who they are and what their place in the world is, are incredibly vulnerable to the influences of those around them.

The parent-child relationship, or lack of it, can shape a child's emotional and psychological health for the rest of their lives. As the developmental psychologist Erik Erikson noted, a child's early years are crucial in forming their identity and sense of trust. This is why, when a child experiences estrangement, the effects are far-reaching and transcend the loss of just a relationship. Estrangement also means the loss of trust and security, which every child should enjoy as they journey through their early years.

These early years, when the brain and sense of self of children are still developing, are so vulnerable to the influence of those around them. Parents, whether present physically or absent emotionally, shape how children view themselves and the world around them. When that emotional bond is cut off, or when that trust is broken, it becomes nearly impossible for the child to feel secure about their place in the world. The absence of love, or the presence of conditional love, can have adverse psychological effects on them even when they become adults.

Let me paint a better picture with the story of Gift, as reported by a social worker in Africa.

(Gift's Story)

Gift did not grow up in the kind of home a child should.

Her parents' relationship was filled with pain, and eventually, they separated because her dad was abusive. As the second child, she should have had someone to lean on, but her elder sister went off course, and that meant Gift had to step up. She became the "big sister" figure even when she was still just a girl herself.

She didn't get to rest. She was her mom's closest support, always there when things got too hard. Her dad also took her as his go-to person. She managed the home as the mother of the house, and was constantly stuck in the middle trying to hold everyone together. It was draining. She was emotionally worn out, physically stressed, and tired of pretending she was okay.

Then, it all got worse. Her dad got arrested and charged to court for a failed business deal. Her mom got seriously sick and ended up in the hospital. At age 20, while in the university, Gift was suddenly the only one holding the family together. She had to keep up with her studies, feed and take care of her younger sister, and even raise her sister's little girl.

There were days she felt like she was going to lose her mind.

One terrible night, their house was burgled. Thieves came in and took everything they could. They almost raped her that night. She fought, cried, and broke down completely. Days later, while in school with her colleagues, she tearfully lamented and said, *"Why can't I just have a normal family? Maybe if my parents were together... maybe none of this would have happened."* From her disposition and the tone of her voice, she obviously longed for peace more than anything.

Eventually, her dad was released from prison. Her mom was also discharged from the hospital, but the happy ending never came. Her dad later became a drug addict, and for Gift, that was the final blow.

She started to sink emotionally but later found a small way to cope.

Gift's Healing Journey

Gift started writing. Poetry. Deep, emotional poems. She would lock herself in a room, play the country music her dad once introduced her to, and write. Sometimes, she did four to five poems in one sitting. Through her tears, she wrote the truth of her heart, and each poem felt like lifting a heavy weight off her chest. For the first time in a long time, she started to feel lighter, and that was the beginning of her healing.

Someone later introduced her to daily Bible reading, too, and she began reading verses that reminded her that she wasn't alone. Scriptures about restoration, peace, and purpose gave her hope. She also found comfort in friends who were going through their pain. They supported each other, and those small conversations helped more than they probably realized.

She also started sharing her poems online. She posted them on websites and on social media. Strangers began to message her, saying, *"This speaks to me," "You wrote my mind," "This poem is relieving,"* and *"Your poem helped me through a hard time."* That made her feel seen and useful, and gave her a sense of purpose.

Bit by bit, Gift started to accept that she couldn't change where she came from, but she could choose where she was going. When the chance came, she left that home. She took her little sister and her sister's daughter with her because she wanted to protect them from more pain. She got married into a kind, loving family that showed her what a real family feels like, and for the first time, she experienced peace, love, and calm.

Now, Gift is using everything she went through to build a new life. The poems that once soaked up her tears became a business. She founded a writing firm where she offers academic, sales, marketing, and business content to clients across the world. She's a consultant to international firms, and more than anything, she is a storyteller with a mission.

She survived the period of pain, found healing, rose from where she found herself, and is now doing well for herself. Gift found ways to not let her background pull her back to the ground, and through her story, young people are reminded that brokenness isn't the end. Healing is real, and even in the darkest moments, you can still find your voice.

Away from this story, let us step aside and consider something really important.

Thankfully, Gift's journey had a happy ending, but that should not be the endpoint. This calls for serious questioning and examination of current parenting styles. Are certain styles more prone to causing estrangement than others? Could it be that a cultural context, or a certain approach to parenting, could make estrangement more likely?

Some cultures, such as African cultures, place a strong emphasis on respect and authority. Children in these cultures are often expected to listen and obey without questioning, which can sometimes create an emotional distance. Yet, this same respect in these cultures can offer the child stability and a sense of security, something that may be different from the more permissive or expressive parenting styles that some Western cultures encourage.

But is one approach better than the other? Could we say that one culture's way of parenting leads to stronger, more emotionally connected relationships?

Let us briefly consider some key parenting styles and also find out if they contribute to the global number of estranged youths, and to what degree, if they do.

Parenting Styles And Youth Estrangement

What if the very approaches we use to raise our children are quietly driving a wedge between generations? An article by Reczek, R. & Bosley-Smith tells us that 26 percent of young adults are estranged from their fathers, while six percent are estranged from their mothers. This rate is alarming, to say the least, and is a fine reason for us to examine how different parenting styles might be contributing to this global phenomenon.

Let me walk you through the four fundamental parenting styles that researchers have identified, and share what the evidence tells us about which approaches lead to thriving children and youths, and which might inadvertently push our kids away.

The Authoritarian Parent:

Picture a household where rules are non-negotiable, questions are discouraged, and compliance is expected without explanation. This is authoritarian parenting in action—high control paired with low warmth. These parents set strict boundaries and expect immediate obedience, often using punishment as their primary tool for managing behavior.

I have watched several authoritarian parents in action, and there's something almost military-like about their approach. There's rarely explanation, minimal emotional support, and little consideration for the child's perspective or feelings.

The research on authoritarian parenting reveals some troubling patterns. This parenting style can lead to higher levels of aggression, while children may also exhibit shyness, social ineptitude, and difficulty making their own decisions (Types of Parenting Styles and Effects on Children, n.d.). Research also shows that children with authoritarian parents perform more poorly than kids with permissive parents (Authoritarian parenting style, n.d.).

Think about that for a moment. Children with virtually no rules actually do better than those with rigid, punitive structures. Why? Because authoritarian parenting often creates what I call external locus children, that means kids who only behave when someone is watching, who struggle to make independent decisions, and who may harbor deep resentment toward authority figures.

The authoritarian parenting style is significantly positively correlated with reduced ability to regulate behavior, reduced self-esteem and self-confidence, low social skills, adjustment difficulties, and depression (Exploring Parenting Styles Patterns, n.d.). These aren't just temporary childhood challenges. They often persist into adulthood and end up creating adults who either rebel completely against structure, or become overly dependent on external validation.

The Authoritative Parent:

Now, let's look at a different picture. Imagine a parent who sets clear expectations but takes time to explain why those expectations exist. They listen to their child's perspective, validate emotions while still maintaining boundaries, and view discipline as teaching rather than punishment. This is authoritative parenting, the style that combines high control with high warmth.

I think of authoritative parents as skilled negotiators. They might say something like, "I understand you're frustrated about your curfew, and I want to hear your thoughts. Here's why this boundary exists, and let's discuss how we might adjust it as you show more responsibility."

The research on authoritative parenting is overwhelmingly positive. Research has shown that children with authoritative parents show the highest levels of academic achievement compared to other parenting styles. They have also demonstrated lower levels of mental illness, drug and alcohol abuse, and aggression into adulthood (Which Parenting Style Is Best?, 2024).

I also like the fact that this parenting style prepares children for the real world. Life requires both structure and flexibility, both following rules and thinking independently. Authoritative parenting mirrors this complexity. Parenting styles that feature warmth and responsiveness (authoritative and permissive) are better overall than the remaining alternatives, and there is evidence favoring authoritative parenting as the "best" style (The authoritative parenting style, 2024).

The Permissive Parent:

On the opposite end of the control spectrum, we find permissive parenting, which is characterized by high warmth but low control. These are the parents who want to be their child's best friend above all else. They're incredibly nurturing and responsive, but they struggle to set and maintain boundaries. Rules are suggestions, consequences are rare, and conflict is avoided at almost any cost.

I have known permissive parents who genuinely believe they are showing love by never saying no. They might say things like, *"Well, if you really don't want to do your homework, I guess that's okay,"* or *"I know the rule is no dessert before dinner, but you seem really upset, so here's some ice cream."*

While these parents have beautiful, warm relationships with their young children, the long-term outcomes are concerning. Children of permissive parents tend to rank low in happiness and self-regulation and are more likely to have problems with authority (Baumrind's Parenting Styles, 2020). So, while permissive parenting offers warmth and open communication, it often lacks boundaries and structure. This can lead to behavioral issues and poor decision-making (Pros and Cons of 4 Parenting Styles, 2025).

Sadly, permissive parents genuinely think they are being kind, but they are often setting their children up for failure in a world that has rules and consequences.

The Uninvolved Parent:

The most heartbreaking parenting style to observe is the uninvolved or neglectful approach (low control and low warmth). These parents are physically present but emotionally absent. They provide basic necessities but offer little guidance, support, or emotional connection. Their children often fend for themselves, making major decisions without adult guidance.

This isn't always intentional neglect. Sometimes these parents are overwhelmed by their struggles, depression, addiction, work stress, or traumatic backgrounds. However, the impact on their children is always profound.

Children of uninvolved parents often demonstrate resilience and may be more self-sufficient than those raised in other parenting styles. However, these skills are typically developed out of necessity. They may struggle with emotional regulation and exhibit less effective coping strategies (Types of Parenting Styles and Effects on Children, n.d.). According to experts, children of uninvolved parents have the worst outcome of all parenting styles. They are the kids who don't feel seen, and in a world that thrives on connection, being invisible to your own parents might be the cruelest experience of all.

Who wins at the end?

After examining decades of research, the evidence is remarkably clear. Youth of authoritative parents had the most favorable development outcomes; authoritarian and permissive parenting were associated with negative developmental outcomes, while outcomes for children of neglectful parents were poorest (Parenting Styles: A Closer Look, 2018).

But why does authoritative parenting work so well? I believe it's because this approach mirrors the complexity of healthy human relationships. It teaches children that love and limits can coexist, that their voices matter, but they're not the only voice that matters, and that respect flows both ways in relationships.

Authoritative parents raise children who are more likely to develop strong emotional regulation skills, maintain healthy relationships throughout life, show academic and professional success, have higher self-esteem and confidence, demonstrate better decision-making abilities, and experience lower rates of mental health issues.

On the flipside, and from my observation and research, authoritarian and uninvolved parenting styles pose the highest risk for eventual estrangement. And here is why:

Authoritarian parents often create children who grow up feeling unheard, controlled, and resentful. As these children become adults and develop their own sense of autonomy, they may view complete separation as the only way to feel free. They've learned that their parents aren't safe people to be vulnerable with, so they protect themselves through distance.

Uninvolved parents create children who grow up feeling unloved and unsupported. These children often become adults who decide they're better off without parents who were never really there anyway. Why maintain a relationship that has never provided comfort or guidance?
Permissive parenting can also contribute to estrangement, but usually for different reasons. Adults who were raised without boundaries sometimes struggle with the give-and-take of adult relationships and may cut off parents who finally try to set limits or express different opinions.

Authoritative parenting, while not immune to estrangement, seems to provide the best foundation for weathering family storms. Children raised this way typically develop the communication skills and emotional resilience needed to work through conflicts rather than simply walking away.

In my opinion, parenting styles aren't a matter of better or worse. It's about understanding the unique strengths and weaknesses of each approach and, more importantly, the need to adapt to the specific emotional needs of each child. For instance, in some cultures, children are expected to learn by doing things independently. This might lead to a sense of autonomy and self-reliance, but without guidance or emotional connection, it can also lead to feelings of isolation or alienation.

Let me give an example.

A young girl named Selena, whom I worked with, had grown up in a group home for at-risk youth. Her mother passed on when she was very young, and her father was completely absent. The only family member she had close contact with was her uncle, but when Selena's uncle sexually assaulted her sister, everything fell apart. Selena, in a fit of anger and confusion, set fire to his house, hoping to destroy the very source of her pain.

As I got to know Selena, it became clear how her world had been shaped by the absence of both a mother and a father figure. Without these foundational relationships, she had to learn how to navigate life on her own, often in ways that were both dangerous and destructive.

The trust she once had in family members was shattered. But could this estrangement have been avoided? Could her uncle have been there for her emotionally instead of perpetuating his cycle of trauma? Could Selena have been taught how to navigate the complex emotions of betrayal without resorting to violence?

The Hidden Roots of Estrangement

So, why does estrangement happen? What causes a parent-child relationship to break down?

Sometimes it's a slow drift, a series of misunderstandings that pile up over time. Other times, it's a much deeper issue, such as addiction, grief, or unresolved trauma.

Let's take addiction, for example. Parents who struggle with substance abuse often find it difficult to provide the emotional support their children need. Research by Empowering Parents (2021) tells us that addiction can cause a parent to neglect the emotional needs of their child, leading the child to feel rejected or unloved.

What often goes unrecognized, though, is that the parents' addiction is also a form of emotional estrangement. The child becomes a victim of neglect, but the parent is often so deep in their own issues that they fail to notice the harm they're causing.

Does this mean that children of parents with addiction are doomed to struggle with estranged relationships themselves? Not necessarily. But it does make the journey to healing more complicated. It means that both the child and the parent must face the underlying issues together. Healing can happen, but it requires a conscious effort and support from the community.

Consider the parents who sever ties with their children. An article by BBC (2022) explored this topic in detail. Often, these parents see estrangement as a form of self-preservation, believing that the relationship is simply too toxic to repair. But the real question becomes, how do we break these cycles? How do we find a way back from estrangement when there's so much emotional pain involved?

In these situations, the estranged child might carry resentment, while the parent may carry guilt. Both sides need healing, but they need it in different ways. This is where faith and religion can offer profound guidance.

Christianity, for example, teaches that forgiveness is essential for healing, both for the one who forgives and the one being forgiven. Psychology Today (2023) points out that many Christian families approach estrangement with a mindset of reconciliation, using prayer and spiritual counseling to repair broken bonds. But it's not always easy, is it? Sometimes, the pain runs so deep that forgiveness feels impossible. In those moments, both the parent and the child need a kind of spiritual and emotional "reset," a new way to look at the situation and reframe the relationship.

The Intersection of Abuse, Addiction, and Estrangement

Addiction, grief, and trauma often sit at the heart of estrangement. These are not just isolated incidents that cause distance between parent and child, but are deep, emotional wounds that have the power to divide a family. Addiction doesn't just steal a parent's ability to care for their child; it often takes away their ability to emotionally engage with anyone, including their own flesh and blood.

A parent consumed by addiction might physically be there, but emotionally, they are far away. Their child becomes a mere bystander in their life, longing for attention and affection that never comes. The erratic nature of addiction means that one day, the parent might be present and loving, and the next, they might be distant, angry, or absent entirely. For a child, this unpredictability is disorienting, and trust becomes a foreign concept.

I have worked with many families where addiction stole the emotional bond, which is the most important part of their relationships. Isn't it one of the most heartbreaking experiences? I have seen mothers whose addiction led them to be forcibly separated from their children, or even have their children apprehended because they were deemed incapable of care. The grief that follows only deepens the cycle of addiction, reinforcing a sense of emotional isolation.

Take Jane's story, which I shared in the previous chapter, for an example. She was separated from her child due to her ongoing meth addiction. Her struggle was with drugs, and with the inability to care for her child. The emotional toll of separation became a new, devastating kind of addiction in itself, one that intertwined with her grief and self-destructive patterns. Jane's child, now an adult, has experienced estrangement as well, a ripple effect of the addiction that ran deep in their family.

This cycle of addiction and separation continues to shape the emotional lives of everyone involved.

The Silent Force of Grief

Grief, though less tangible, is just as powerful in creating emotional distance. When a parent is grieving, whether from the loss of a loved one, the breakdown of their own mental health, or personal setbacks, they may retreat into themselves, building a wall between them and their child. Grief becomes an emotional barrier, one that is difficult, if not impossible, to overcome.

For a child, growing up with a parent who is emotionally absent due to grief means grappling with a loss that can't quite be named. The parent isn't gone physically, but emotionally, they may be locked away in their world of sadness and reflection. A child, too young to process their own grief, is left to navigate the painful reality that their parent is unavailable and unable to provide the support or love they so desperately need.

In Jane's case, grief wasn't just something she experienced after the separation from her child. Her grief was layered, tied to the sorrow of losing herself to addiction, of losing the mother she longed to be. This grief often fueled her continued struggles, pushing her further into isolation and addiction. It was a cycle of loss that felt almost impossible to break, with each wave of grief reinforcing her emotional withdrawal.

Healing from grief, especially when tied to addiction, requires immense effort. It is not enough to simply move on; it's about learning to process loss, to find a way back to the self, and ultimately, to create a path toward reconnection. For someone like Jane, the healing journey might have seemed overwhelming at times. But through therapy, support, and a willingness to face the harsh truths of her past, there was a possibility of rebuilding, one small step at a time.

The Place Of Trauma In Estrangement

I call this the invisible wound because parents who have experienced deep trauma (whether from childhood abuse, war, loss, or ongoing systemic oppression) may be unable to provide the nurturing their children need because they, too, are consumed by their unresolved pain.

Children and youth of traumatized parents often inherit the emotional weight of their parents' experiences, whether they are conscious of it or not. When a parent's trauma is left unaddressed, it manifests as emotional withdrawal, an inability to connect, and sometimes even destructive behaviors. The emotional distance that comes from living with a parent who has never healed from their trauma can feel like an endless, suffocating silence for the child. They are often left to navigate a world without emotional guidance, feeling lost in the shadow of someone else's pain.

In Jane's case, trauma was a constant thread throughout her upbringing. She, too, had been raised by a parent who struggled with unresolved pain. Jane's mother, like many before her, was affected by generational trauma, shaped by a history of abuse, neglect, and poverty that stunted her emotional growth. These unresolved wounds carried over into Jane's life, deepening her struggle with addiction and grief. Living in a lower socio-economic environment, surrounded by layers of systemic neglect and abuse, Jane was bound by the weight of a trauma that was both inherited and perpetuated.

Yet, trauma is not the end of the story. It is not the final chapter. In fact, it can be a starting point for healing. Recognizing the influence of generational trauma in Jane's life allowed her to begin the long process of confronting her past. Through understanding her family's pain, Jane was able to take the first steps toward breaking free from the cycle and forging a different path for herself and, perhaps, for her children.

Healing from trauma isn't easy, and it isn't quick. It requires unraveling layers of pain that have been built up over a lifetime, but the act of healing is deeply personal. It begins with confronting the root causes of one's pain and finding the courage to reimagine a life without the shadow of that pain dictating every decision.

But what happens when addiction, grief, and trauma converge in a family?

This is the devastating reality that many children and young people face—living in homes where multiple forms of emotional abandonment coexist.

A parent might be battling addiction while still carrying the grief of past losses, all while never having dealt with their childhood trauma. The emotional chaos that this creates within the home is almost impossible to escape. Children grow up in a state of perpetual emotional neglect, never truly feeling safe, loved, or seen.

And the impact is of no small measure.

These children often grow up to struggle with their sense of trust and self-worth. How can they trust others when they were never able to trust the one person they should have been able to rely on the most? How can they feel secure in their relationships when the very foundation of emotional connection was never built? The longer the estrangement continues, the deeper these emotional scars become. Healing from this kind of emotional trauma is not just about time. It's about confronting the damage head-on and learning to rebuild trust in a world that feels unsafe.

For many children, estrangement doesn't occur in isolation. It is often connected to deeper issues such as abuse or neglect. The Vanier Institute (2020) found that among Indigenous circles, which include First Nations and Métis families, parent-child separations were sometimes the result of systemic issues like poverty, historical trauma, and substance abuse. These external factors often lead to the disintegration of the family unit, leaving children to deal with the emotional fallout alone.

However, the key here is trust. Trust takes time to build, but it can also be easily broken. And when a child has been betrayed by someone they loved, whether it's a parent, a guardian, or an extended family member, rebuilding that trust becomes one of the hardest challenges in the healing process.

Indigenous View on Estrangement

When we consider estrangement in the context of Indigenous communities, the differences between urban and remote settings can significantly influence the nature of these emotional rifts. Indigenous communities often prioritize collective values (family, community, respect, and shared identity) above individualism. In remote, northern areas, where traditions and customs are more deeply ingrained, children might grow up with a stronger sense of connection to their heritage and to their parents.

These traditional ways provide stability and a sense of belonging that can help cushion the blow of emotional estrangement. However, even in these settings, systemic issues like poverty, trauma from colonization, or substance abuse can fracture families, leading to estrangement.

But what happens when an Indigenous child is raised in an urban setting? Urbanization brings a different set of challenges. Proximity to traditional values may weaken in cities, and young people might find themselves caught between two worlds: the world of their ancestral culture and the pressures of modern, individualistic society. The disconnection from their cultural roots—often due to the pressures of assimilating or surviving in an urban environment—can make estrangement feel even more isolating.

When a child feels torn between these worlds, their emotional needs may go unmet, further exacerbating feelings of abandonment.

For Indigenous youth, healing is deeply connected to community and culture and not just a personal journey. Reconnecting with their heritage, with elders, and with cultural practices can be crucial in bridging the gap between estranged relationships. But when those cultural connections are distant or disrupted by urban life, healing becomes more complex.

Afrocentric View on Estrangement

In many African and Black communities, family relationships are often framed by cultural expectations of respect, loyalty, and authority. Discipline and respect are key components of the parent-child relationship, but in some instances, these values can unintentionally create emotional distance.

When children or youths grow up in environments where emotional expression is secondary to respect and obedience, they may struggle with connecting to their parents on a deeper, more vulnerable level. The emotional warmth that they may crave can feel absent, replaced by the cultural expectation of compliance and silence.

Moreover, historical trauma, stemming from colonization, slavery, and ongoing systemic oppression, can cast a long shadow over Black and African families. Parents who have inherited generational trauma may be emotionally unavailable to their children, not because they don't love them, but because their own wounds have never healed. The emotional scars left by centuries of injustice and abuse are not easily healed, and they can prevent parents from fully engaging with their children in the way they need. When a parent is overwhelmed by their own trauma, they often lack the emotional resources to guide or nurture their child, further deepening the estrangement.

Healing in this context is multifaceted. Faith, community, and cultural pride are often central to the healing process. The support of extended family, religious institutions, or African-centered therapeutic practices can provide the necessary framework to rebuild emotional connections. But the question remains: How do we heal when so much of our emotional inheritance is laced with trauma? How can Black and African communities reconcile the scars of the past while still offering a healthy future for their children?

Western View on Estrangement

When we examine estrangement through a Western lens, individual autonomy and personal choice emerge as the dominant themes shaping how we understand family disconnection. Western societies, particularly in North America and Europe, champion the idea that each person has the right to choose their relationships, even with family members. This individualistic framework views estrangement as a legitimate option when family relationships become harmful or unfulfilling. In this context, cutting ties isn't seen as failure but as an act of self-preservation and personal growth.

Family estrangement is sometimes the result of one significant family conflict. But often, it is an accumulation of family conflict that eventually leads to parental alienation, reflecting the Western tendency to analyze and categorize emotional experiences. The emphasis on personal boundaries, mental health awareness, and trauma-informed thinking has created a culture where young adults feel empowered and are often encouraged to distance themselves from relationships that feel toxic or limiting.

Healing in Western contexts typically involves individual therapy to help children and youths navigate the emotional impact of the estrangement, and heal past trauma leading to their decision. While this individual focus can provide important insights and emotional relief, it may not address the deeper cultural patterns that make estrangement seem like the only viable option.

As we look across different cultures and contexts, one truth becomes clear: estrangement is not just a personal issue—it is a systemic, cultural, and emotional problem that requires collective healing. Whether through reclaiming cultural identity, confronting addiction and grief, or understanding the deep scars left by historical trauma, the journey to healing is complex, but not impossible. It requires not just individual reflection but a community effort to provide the emotional support, understanding, and guidance that children and parents need to rebuild trust and reconnect.

Healing and Rebuilding Connections

I'm sure the question on everyone's mind now is: How do we heal? How do we rebuild the relationships that have been broken by estrangement, addiction, abuse, or grief?

For the children and youth who find themselves disconnected from their parents, the journey to healing begins with understanding. Greater Good Berkeley (2021) emphasizes the importance of emotional education—teaching children to understand and express their feelings in healthy ways. But this cannot happen in a vacuum. For youth to heal, they need safe spaces, emotionally available adults, and mentors who can offer them guidance.

Similarly, parents who have been estranged from their children need to take steps toward reconciliation. This might mean therapy, open conversations, or even just learning to listen with empathy. The hardest part for many parents is recognizing their role in the estrangement. Psychology Today (2023) suggests that parents must be willing to admit their mistakes and take ownership of the damage done. This is often the first step toward repairing the relationship.

From the perspectives of Indigenous, Western, and Afrocentric healing traditions, the path to reconciliation is rooted in both individual and community efforts. In African communities, the focus often lies on collective healing—restoring harmony within the family unit and community at large. In Western traditions, therapy and personal reflection are typically emphasized. Indigenous approaches often involve ritual and spiritual practices, which acknowledge the trauma while also creating a pathway for healing.

For caregivers and professionals working with estranged youths, the work of healing is not just about fixing a broken relationship. It's about providing the tools for emotional resilience. A young person who has experienced estrangement needs to know they are not alone, that there are adults who care and are willing to listen. As IF Studies (2022) discusses, foster parents and guardians have a crucial role in helping these young people rebuild trust in the adults around them.

For parents who are still in contact with their children, the key to moving forward is humility. Healing doesn't happen overnight, but it can begin with small steps. Maybe it's simply asking, "How are you?" or offering a listening ear. Rebuilding a relationship takes time, but it can happen, one conversation at a time.

And so, we have come full circle. What is the way forward?

As we've seen throughout this chapter, healing from estranged parent-child relationships is a delicate, often painful journey. But it's a journey that's full of potential for growth, understanding, and reconciliation. Whether you're a child seeking to repair a fractured relationship, a parent looking for ways to reconnect, or a caregiver working with youth who have faced these struggles, there are ways to take actionable steps toward healing.

Now, I want to guide you through a few activities that can help facilitate reflection, healing, and a deeper understanding of this complex topic. These exercises are designed not only to help you process your own feelings but also to build the skills needed to navigate the often difficult waters of estranged relationships.

Self-Reflection: Understanding Your Own Story

Start by reflecting on your experiences and the relationships that have shaped you. This is a deeply personal activity, but it's important to see the connections between your past and your present relationships.

Activity: The "Family Tree" Reflection

Instructions: Take a moment to draw a simple family tree. Include the people who have had the greatest impact on your life, both positive and negative. This may include biological parents, adoptive parents, mentors, or guardians. As you fill in the tree, consider how these relationships have shaped your view of yourself, your identity, and your trust in others.

Once your tree is drawn, take a few minutes to answer the following questions:

- How did these relationships affect your emotional growth and development?
- Were there any patterns in these relationships (positive or negative) that seem to repeat through generations?
- Are there any unresolved issues with any of the people in your tree? What steps could you take to address them?

Reflection: How do the experiences in your family tree connect to your current relationships, especially the one with your parent or guardian?

Research from *"A Broken Bond: The Pain of Mother-Child Estrangement"* (IF Studies, 2022) tells us that estranged parent-child relationships are often influenced by generational patterns. Parents who had unresolved issues with their parents might struggle with similar challenges in their relationships with their children. By recognizing these patterns, we can break the cycle and create healthier connections.

Seeking Forgiveness and Offering Grace

Forgiveness is often seen as the final step in healing estranged relationships, but it's rarely that simple. It's not just about saying "I forgive you"; it's about letting go of resentment, embracing vulnerability, and offering grace to one another.

Activity: The Forgiveness Letter

Instructions: Write a letter to your estranged parent, guardian, or child. This letter is for you alone; you may choose to send it or not, but it will serve as an emotional release. In your letter, express:

- The pain you feel from the estrangement.
- The ways in which you've been hurt, but also the ways you've grown because of this experience.
- Your desire for healing and what steps you're willing to take to rebuild the relationship.

If you feel it's appropriate, you can also write a letter from the perspective of your parent or child. Imagine what they might say to you in their own words, and let this give you new insights into their feelings.

Reflection: Writing forgiveness letters is about letting go of negative emotions and creating space for healing. It's about freeing yourself from the cycle of pain and resentment, whether or not the relationship is repaired.

Rebuilding Trust: Small, Consistent Actions

Healing doesn't happen all at once. Sometimes, the best way to rebuild a relationship is through small, consistent actions that show care and commitment.

Activity: The "Trust-Building Steps" List

Instructions: Write down small actions that could help rebuild trust. For example, if you're a parent, you might commit to listening more patiently or sending your child a message of affirmation. If you're a child, you might set boundaries around communication, or express your feelings when something hurts.

Write down five specific, achievable steps you can take. It is important that these steps are actionable and not overwhelming. Some examples might include:

- Parent: I will ask my child how they're feeling, without offering advice or judgment.

- Child: I will be open to talking, even if it's difficult, and express my feelings honestly.

Self Reflection: Rebuilding trust is a long-term process, and it requires effort from both sides. These small steps are about creating a foundation of mutual respect and understanding.

Healing from estranged relationships is neither a simple nor a quick process. It may be messy, emotional, and, at times, excruciating. But as we've seen through these exercises and discussions, healing is possible. Whether you're a parent or a child, a caregiver or a mentor, taking responsibility, being vulnerable, and embracing empathy are essential components in moving forward.

As you continue this journey, remember that healing takes time, and progress may not assume a straight path. Each small step you take toward reconciliation, whether in action or in thought, is a victory. And though the past may never be fully erased, it is through these difficult, brave conversations and actions that we pave the way for a healthier, more connected future.

CHAPTER SEVEN
HEALING FOR CHILDREN & YOUTH WITH DISABILITIES

"If you cannot change the circumstance, then change the way you look at your circumstance." - Senator Crystal Asige

I watched a rebroadcast of Senator Crystal Asige as she stood before the One Young World Summit audience, her hands trembling slightly as she adjusted the microphone. What followed was a story that would resonate far beyond that auditorium—a testament to the resilience that defines so many young people living with disabilities around the world.

Crystal's journey into visual impairment began in 2010 with what was supposed to be a routine 40-minute eye surgery. Instead, she found herself under general anesthesia for two grueling hours, emerging not with restored sight but with even less vision than before.

The diagnosis was devastating. She had what her doctor grimly called "glaucoma the remix", which is an aggressive form that affects Black Africans more severely due to the pigmentation of their eyes. The prognosis revealed that she would likely be completely blind by age 25.

Since high school, Crystal had been slowly, gradually losing her sight, but she never fully understood why. No one in her family had experienced anything similar. What followed were over 20 different procedures, each one a desperate attempt to reclaim even tiny fragments of the vision that had slipped away. But as a teenager on the small island of Mombasa, Crystal wasn't just navigating the physical reality of going blind; she was confronting a world steeped in discrimination and traditional prejudices toward disability.

The part of Crystal's story that is not just striking but forms the basis for the introduction of this chapter is where she said, *"It's one thing to go blind, but it's another thing to go blind in a society filled with discrimination and traditional prejudices."* How true. She further added a powerful quote, which says, *"If all you see is what you see, then you don't see all there is to be seen."*

Crystal's story points to a reality that millions of children and young people with disabilities face worldwide, one that demands our urgent attention and compassionate response. While her journey speaks to remarkable individual resilience, it also reveals the systemic barriers and societal attitudes that continue to marginalize young people with disabilities across the globe.

According to UNICEF, approximately 240 million children worldwide live with disabilities, nearly one in ten children globally. These young people are among the most marginalized and excluded in society, facing barriers that extend far beyond their specific impairments. They are significantly less likely to attend school, access healthcare, or participate fully in their communities.

In education alone, children with disabilities face staggering inequities. The UNESCO Institute for Statistics reports that children with disabilities are more than twice as likely to be out of school compared to their peers without disabilities. In some regions, this disparity is even more pronounced. Do you know that in Sub-Saharan Africa, for instance, children with disabilities are up to five times more likely never to enter school at all?

Now, "disability" is that word that holds many meanings shaped by context, culture, and experience.

Some define it by visible physical impairments, while others define it by conditions invisible to the eye, like neurodevelopmental disorders, learning differences, sensory sensitivities, chronic health conditions, and more. The truth is, disability spans across every human spectrum. It can be visible, invisible, temporary, permanent, mild, or profound. It can even go undiagnosed for years.

I hope you know that in some cultures, what we recognize as a disability may not even be acknowledged as such. A child struggling with focus or sensitivity to noise might be seen as disobedient, lazy, or simply "difficult." Labels are easily handed out. But recognition? Understanding? That takes time, awareness, and compassion.

In my work within institutional settings, particularly with children and youths, I have had the privilege—and the heartache—of seeing these nuances unfold firsthand. I have learned that it is often easier to spot developmental differences in children than in adults.

A child who is not walking, talking, or socializing at expected developmental milestones often raises early concern. But an adult who has spent years masking symptoms, adapting, or going undiagnosed might be misunderstood entirely and even labeled as rude, difficult, or unstable sometimes.

Take ADHD (Attention-Deficit/Hyperactivity Disorder), for instance. Or autism. These conditions sit on a wide spectrum and present differently in different people. While they are being recognized more today than ever before, in many communities and cultures, they are still met with suspicion, denial, or blame. Some parents I've worked with had never even heard of these terms before arriving in a new country; now imagine the fear and confusion they feel when told their child may need special support.

And I'll be honest. I've made mistakes too.

There were times I didn't recognize someone's disability. I judged their behavior, interpreted their words harshly, and assumed the worst. With time and reflection, I've grown. I've learned to look beyond the surface. And to those I failed to understand before, I am sorry. Not just on my behalf, but on behalf of a society that often only acknowledges what it can clearly see.

I am doing this in recognition of the fact that healing can only be accelerated if and when parents, guardians, medical professionals, and we as social workers approach these children and youth the right way. So, is there a right or wrong way to go about this? Let's find out.

The Wrong Versus The Right Approach

In my years of working with families, educators, and communities, I have seen how our manner of approach can either build bridges or create walls for children and youth with disabilities. The difference between healing and harm often lies not in our intentions, but in our understanding and methods.

Let me walk you through some of the most common yet damaging practices I've encountered and show you how we can transform them into approaches that truly serve these remarkable young people.

The Language We Use

The Wrong Way: I cringe every time I hear someone say, "What's wrong with that child?" or refer to a young person as "suffering from autism" or being "confined to a wheelchair." These phrases, though often spoken without malice, immediately frame disability as something tragic, something that diminishes a person's worth.

The Right Way: Instead, I encourage people to use person-first language. Say "a child with autism" rather than "an autistic child." Replace "suffers from cerebral palsy" with "has cerebral palsy." Instead of "confined to a wheelchair," try "uses a wheelchair." This simple shift acknowledges that the person comes first, and their disability is just one aspect of who they are, not their defining characteristic.

The Pity Trap

The Wrong Way: I've watched well-meaning adults approach children with disabilities with exaggerated sympathy, speaking in overly soft tones and treating them as fragile beings who need constant protection. This approach, while coming from a place of care, actually robs these children of their agency and dignity.

The Right Way: Treat children and youth with disabilities as you would any other young person, showing them respect, genuine interest, and age-appropriate expectations. Celebrate their achievements without making them feel like heroes for simply existing. Remember, they're not looking for pity, but authentic connection and opportunity.

The Assumption Game

The Wrong Way: Too often, I see people making assumptions about what children and youth with disabilities can or cannot do. They speak over them to their caregivers, assume they can't understand, or automatically exclude them from activities without even asking.

The Right Way: Always speak directly to the young person first, regardless of their disability. Ask them about their needs, preferences, and capabilities rather than assuming. If they need assistance communicating, they'll let you know or indicate through their caregiver. Give them the same respect and autonomy you'd offer any other young person.

The Inspiration Objectification Problem

The Wrong Way: I have grown uncomfortable with how society often uses the stories of children and youth with disabilities solely to motivate others or make non-disabled people feel better about their own lives. Comments like "If they can do it, so can you!" reduce these young people to mere objects of inspiration.

The Right Way: Celebrate achievements genuinely and in context. If a young person with a disability accomplishes something noteworthy, recognize it for what it is, not because it's surprising given their disability, but because it's genuinely impressive. Let their stories inspire action toward inclusion and justice, not just warm feelings.

Educational Segregation

The Wrong Way: The practice of automatically placing children with disabilities in separate classrooms or schools, away from their peers, continues in many places. This segregation, often justified as "specialized care," actually limits these children's social development and reinforces the idea that they don't belong in mainstream society.

The Right Way: Embrace inclusive education wherever possible. This means providing necessary supports and accommodations within regular classrooms, training teachers to work with diverse learners, and creating environments where all children learn together. Research consistently shows that inclusion benefits everyone. Children with disabilities develop better social skills and academic outcomes, while their peers develop empathy and acceptance.

The Medical Model Trap

The Wrong Way: I've also seen many situations where children and youth with disabilities are viewed primarily through a medical lens, more like problems to be fixed, conditions to be cured, or deficits to be remedied. This approach focuses solely on what's "wrong" rather than recognizing the whole person.

The Right Way: Adopt a social model of disability that recognizes barriers in the environment, not just limitations in the person. While medical support remains important, focus equally on removing environmental barriers, providing appropriate accommodations, and building on strengths and interests.

Discrimination and Prejudice

The Wrong Way: Perhaps the most damaging of all are the outright discriminatory practices I still encounter: children being denied admission to schools, youth being excluded from sports teams or social activities, families being asked to leave public spaces, or young people facing bullying that goes unaddressed by authorities.

The Right Way: Actively work to create inclusive spaces and challenge discriminatory attitudes wherever you encounter them. This means advocating for policy changes, calling out inappropriate behavior when you see it, and consistently demonstrating through your own actions that everyone belongs. Remember, inclusion is more about justice and human rights, rather than being nice.

Understanding Different Types of Disabilities

To truly support children and youth with disabilities, I believe we must first understand what they are experiencing. Let's look at some of the most common disabilities likely to be encountered, and let me help you recognize the signs, and also understand the factors that contribute to them.

Attention Deficit Hyperactivity Disorder (ADHD)

When I began working with children who have ADHD, I quickly learned that this neurological condition affects much more than just attention. These young people have differences in brain development that impact their ability to focus, control impulses, and regulate their activity levels.

You might notice a child with ADHD having difficulty sitting still during activities, frequently interrupting conversations, or seeming to daydream even when spoken to directly. They might start tasks enthusiastically but struggle to complete them, or appear disorganized despite their best efforts.

ADHD often has genetic components. If a parent has ADHD, their child has a higher likelihood of having it too. Environmental factors like premature birth, exposure to toxins during pregnancy, or brain injuries can also contribute. What's crucial to understand is that ADHD isn't caused by poor parenting, too much screen time, or eating too much sugar, despite what some people believe.

Autism Spectrum Disorder

Autism is exactly what its name suggests—a spectrum. I've worked with children (who have autism) who are brilliant mathematicians but struggle with social conversations, others who are incredibly creative but find changes in routine overwhelming, and still others who communicate beautifully through art but find verbal communication challenging.

Signs of autism typically include difficulties with social communication and interaction, along with restricted or repetitive behaviors and interests. You might notice a child who avoids eye contact, has intense interests in specific topics, engages in repetitive movements like hand-flapping, or becomes distressed by changes in routine or sensory experiences like loud noises or certain textures.

Research suggests autism has strong genetic components, though environmental factors during pregnancy might also play a role. What we know for certain is that autism is not caused by vaccines, parenting style, or anything the family did wrong (a myth that has caused tremendous unnecessary guilt for families).

Hearing Loss and Deafness

Hearing loss in children can range from mild difficulties hearing certain sounds to complete deafness. Some children are born with hearing loss, while others develop it due to illness, injury, or exposure to loud sounds. You might notice a child who doesn't respond when called, asks for things to be repeated frequently, turns up the volume on devices, or seems to rely heavily on visual cues during conversations. Some children might have speech that's difficult to understand or might be delayed in developing spoken language.

Causes include genetic factors, complications during birth, infections like meningitis, or chronic ear infections. Some medications can also affect hearing. Early identification and intervention are crucial. Many children with hearing loss can develop excellent language skills with appropriate support, whether through hearing aids, cochlear implants, or sign language.

Blindness and Visual Impairment

Like Crystal Asige's experience shows us, vision loss can occur at any age and for various reasons. Some children are born blind or with low vision, while others, like Crystal, experience gradual vision loss over time.

Signs might include difficulty seeing objects at a distance, bumping into things frequently, holding books very close to their face, or covering one eye to see better. Some children might be sensitive to light or have difficulty seeing in dim lighting.

Causes range from genetic conditions to premature birth complications, infections, injuries, or diseases like glaucoma. What's important to remember is that blindness or low vision doesn't limit intelligence or potential. These children simply need different tools and techniques to access information and navigate their world.

Cerebral Palsy

Cerebral palsy affects movement and posture due to damage to the developing brain, typically before or during birth. I've worked with young people who have mild cerebral palsy that barely affects their daily activities, and others who need significant support with movement and communication.

You might notice difficulties with coordination, muscle stiffness or looseness, tremors, or challenges with fine motor skills like writing or buttoning clothes. Some children might walk with an unusual gait, use mobility aids, or have difficulty with speech.

The most common causes include brain damage from lack of oxygen during birth, infections during pregnancy, premature birth, or brain injuries in early childhood. While cerebral palsy affects movement, it doesn't necessarily affect intelligence, as many people with cerebral palsy have typical cognitive abilities but may need alternative ways to communicate or demonstrate their knowledge.

Learning Disabilities

Learning disabilities affect how the brain processes information, making it challenging to acquire certain academic skills despite typical intelligence. The most common is dyslexia, which affects reading, but some disabilities impact mathematics, writing, or information processing.

You might notice a bright child who struggles significantly with reading despite extra help, has difficulty with math concepts that seem simple, or can explain ideas verbally but struggles to get them down on paper.

These children often work much harder than their peers to achieve the same results.

Learning disabilities often run in families and involve differences in brain structure and function. They're not caused by lack of intelligence, poor teaching, or not trying hard enough. With appropriate support and teaching methods, children with learning disabilities can be very successful academically.

Intellectual Disabilities

Intellectual disabilities involve limitations in both intellectual functioning and adaptive behavior, which are the everyday social and practical skills we all need to live independently. The severity can range from mild to severe.

You might notice delays in reaching developmental milestones, difficulties with problem-solving or abstract thinking, challenges learning new skills, or trouble with daily living skills like dressing or managing money. However, people with intellectual disabilities have the same emotional needs as everyone else and can form meaningful relationships and contribute to their communities.

Causes include genetic conditions like Down Syndrome, complications during pregnancy or birth, illnesses, or environmental factors like exposure to toxins. Early intervention and ongoing support can significantly improve outcomes and quality of life.

Physical Disabilities

Physical disabilities affect mobility, dexterity, or other aspects of physical functioning. They might be present from birth or acquired through injury or illness. The range is enormous—from children who use wheelchairs to those with limb differences to others with conditions affecting muscle strength or coordination.

Signs depend entirely on the specific condition but might include difficulty walking, limited range of motion, muscle weakness, or differences in limb development. What's crucial to understand is that physical disabilities don't typically affect intelligence or emotional development.

Causes include genetic conditions, complications during birth, accidents, illnesses like muscular dystrophy, or amputations due to various medical reasons. Many physical disabilities can be well-managed with appropriate medical care, adaptive equipment, and environmental modifications.

The Reality of Comorbidity

One aspect of disability that many people do not fully grasp is comorbidity, which is the presence of multiple conditions in the same person. In my experience working with children and youth with disabilities, comorbidity is quite common, and understanding it is crucial for providing appropriate support.

Imagine a young person who has both asthma and ADHD, or someone with cerebral palsy who also has a learning disability. Each condition brings its own challenges, but when they occur together, the impact isn't simply additive but complex and interconnected.

For children and youths, comorbidity can create what I call a "perfect storm" of challenges. A child with both autism and anxiety, for example, might find the social demands of school overwhelming, not just because of communication differences, but because anxiety amplifies every social interaction. A young person with both ADHD and a learning disability might struggle not only with attention but also with processing information, making traditional teaching methods doubly ineffective.

What makes this particularly challenging for families and educators is that the symptoms of different conditions can mask or mimic each other. A child's difficulty focusing might be attributed to ADHD when it's actually anxiety, or behavioral challenges might be seen as defiance when they're actually communication attempts by a child with both autism and an intellectual disability.

Supporting young people with comorbid conditions requires a holistic approach. We can't address one condition while ignoring the others. Instead, we need comprehensive assessment, coordinated care between different specialists, and individualized support plans that account for the full picture of a young person's needs and

Comorbidity is a reminder to us that every child with a disability is unique. Even children with the same diagnosed conditions will have different experiences, different needs, and different strengths. This is why I always emphasize the importance of getting to know each young person as an individual, rather than making assumptions based on diagnostic labels.

The presence of multiple conditions doesn't diminish a young person's potential. It simply means they need more thoughtful, comprehensive support to reach it. And when we provide that support effectively, these young people often surprise us with their resilience, creativity, and achievements.

Yet even here, biases creep in. Some disabilities, like cancer or cerebral palsy, elicit empathy and urgency. Others, like obesity or eating disorders, are often seen as self-inflicted or controllable. The stigma can be more harsh. Even ADHD, when misunderstood, can be misinterpreted as "bad parenting" or "bad behavior." It's unfair, painful, and wrong.

Every child, regardless of the visibility or "severity" of their condition, deserves to be seen, heard, and supported. But how we view these children often depends on our lenses: our upbringing, our cultural beliefs, and the societal standards we inherited.

Let's not pretend healing is simple either. What does healing even mean? Is it about curing a condition? Making someone "normal"? Or is it something deeper? I have come to believe that healing is a journey. It's progress. It's an adaptation. And sometimes, it's simply the softening of judgment in others.

Let me tell you about Halima (not her real name).

(Halima's Story)

She was three years old when I met her. A bright, sweet little girl in a home and school setting, who had noticeable delays in walking and speaking. Her diagnosis wasn't clear-cut—like many children her age, she was still developing. She was placed in a group with other children, many of whom were diagnosed with autism.

I was trained in Applied Behavior Analysis (ABA), a widely used approach that emphasizes structured activities, positive reinforcement, and goal-based interventions. And yes, ABA can be incredibly helpful in shaping certain skills. But over time, I noticed something.

When Halima was left to play freely, something beautiful happened. She relaxed, expressed herself, and laughed. The strict structure didn't always serve her; sometimes it felt like it served the system more than the child.

Her parents, who were new immigrants and still finding their footing in a foreign land, were kind, curious, and deeply devoted. They asked questions that many professionals overlooked. They weren't familiar with these developmental terms, yet their intuition was spot-on. They knew what made their daughter feel safe and joyful.

And despite the structure I was meant to follow, I tried to meet them halfway. I listened. I learned. And I'll never forget Halima's small victories—the first time she communicated her needs, the way her eyes sparkled during unstructured play. That experience taught me more than any textbook ever could.

But then, not every memory is gentle.

In that same setting, I witnessed the undercurrents of cultural bias and racial tension. I wasn't always the preferred caregiver—not because of my skill or dedication, but because of my race or cultural background. I saw families gravitate toward caregivers who "looked like them" or "understood their culture." Sometimes, staff stuck rigidly to protocols out of fear—fear of losing their jobs or fear of stepping out of line. It was disheartening, and yes, it left scars.

These moments still live in me. Some I wish I could forget. Others I treasure because they made me better.

If there's one thing I want you to take from this chapter, it's this: disability is not always found in a piece. It is layered, lived, and experienced differently by each person. It is shaped by biology, yes, but also by society, culture, family, and time.

We must widen our lens, see what isn't visible, and listen to what isn't spoken.

Western Approaches To Healing

Healing for children and youth with disabilities, within the Western framework, often focuses on maximizing functional abilities, developing coping strategies, and building self-advocacy skills. I've seen incredible results from occupational therapy that helps a child with cerebral palsy learn to write, speech therapy that gives voice to a young person with autism, or cognitive behavioral therapy that helps a teenager with anxiety manage their emotions.

The Western approach also emphasizes independence and self-determination. It teaches young people with disabilities to understand their rights, advocate for accommodations, and take control of their own lives. This perspective values individual achievement, personal growth, and the development of skills that will help someone succeed in a competitive, individualistic society.

What I appreciate about this approach is its commitment to evidence-based practice and continuous improvement. Treatments are tested, refined, and improved based on research outcomes. There's also a strong emphasis on early intervention, that is, catching challenges early and providing intensive support when the brain is most adaptable.

However, I've also learned that the Western approach sometimes focuses so intensely on fixing deficits that it can overlook the importance of community, cultural identity, and spiritual well-being. It can also place tremendous pressure on families to pursue intensive interventions that may not align with their values or circumstances.

Indigenous Approaches To Healing

In Indigenous traditions I have encountered, disability is often viewed not as a personal deficit but as a different way of being that may carry special gifts or purposes. Some Indigenous communities understand certain disabilities as indicating that a person has been chosen for a special spiritual role or possesses unique insights.

The healing process emphasizes restoration of balance between the individual and their community, between the person and the natural world, and between the physical, emotional, mental, and spiritual aspects of well-being. Relationship is everything in holistic approaches to Aboriginal child and youth mental health, and this principle extends to supporting young people with disabilities.

Traditional ceremonies, storytelling, and cultural practices help young people find their place and purpose. When a child with a disability participates in cultural activities alongside their peers, when they hear stories of ancestors who overcame challenges, and when they experience the unconditional acceptance of their community, something profound happens that goes beyond what any individual therapy can achieve.

Indigenous cultures also emphasize intergenerational healing—understanding that trauma and resilience are passed down through generations, and that healing for one young person can have ripple effects throughout their family and community.

Afrocentric Approaches To Healing

In Ubuntu philosophy, a person's worth isn't determined by their individual abilities or achievements but by their inherent humanity and their connection to the community. Afrocentric interventions built on cultural values and practices have greater potential to be acceptable, can foster integration, and are likely to be more sustainable.

I've seen this philosophy in action in African communities where children with disabilities aren't segregated or pitied but are understood as full members of the community with their own roles to play. The focus isn't on what they can't do, but on how the community can adapt to include everyone.

Afrocentric community health care can disrupt systemic anti-Black racism and related health inequities by providing holistic, culturally appropriate support that addresses not just individual needs but community well-being. This approach recognizes that healing cannot happen in isolation but requires the active participation of the entire community.

The beautiful thing about this perspective is how it shifts the burden of adaptation from the individual to the community. Instead of asking, *"How can this child learn to fit in?"* it asks, *"How can we change our community so everyone belongs?"*

Religious Views On Healing

Many families I work with find deep comfort and strength in their Christian faith or other religious traditions. These perspectives offer unique insights into healing that emphasize spiritual well-being, divine purpose, and unconditional love.

From a Christian perspective, every child is created in the image of God with inherent worth and dignity that isn't diminished by disability. I've seen families find tremendous peace in the belief that their child's life has purpose and meaning, even when that purpose may look different from societal expectations.

Many Christian communities emphasize the concept of the body of Christ, which sells the idea that everyone has gifts to contribute and that the community is incomplete without every member. This can be profoundly healing for young people with disabilities who have been made to feel like burdens or less valuable than their peers.

The emphasis on grace as unmerited love and acceptance can be particularly powerful for families dealing with the shame and stigma that unfortunately still surround disability in many communities. When families experience genuine acceptance in their faith communities, it can transform their entire perspective on their child's disability.

Prayer, spiritual practices, and faith community support provide coping resources that complement medical and educational interventions. Many families draw strength from their belief that they're not facing challenges alone and that there's a greater purpose at work even in difficult circumstances.

However, I have also encountered problematic religious responses to disability—from the belief that disability is punishment for sin to the pressure to seek miraculous healing rather than practical support. The healthiest religious communities I know balance faith in divine healing with practical action to support families and remove barriers to participation.

Religious healing often emphasizes hope, not just hope for a cure or improvement, but hope for purpose, belonging, and eternal significance. This can sustain families through difficult times, and help young people with disabilities develop resilience and self-worth that goes beyond their functional abilities.

In all of these, we must understand that these different approaches to healing aren't mutually exclusive. They can complement and strengthen each other. A young person might benefit from Western medical interventions while also finding identity and belonging through cultural practices, community support, and spiritual faith.

What is more important is respecting each family's values and choices, while ensuring that young people have access to all the resources that might help them thrive. Sometimes this means helping families navigate between different systems of care, translating between different worldviews, or advocating for culturally responsive services within mainstream systems.

The Way Forward For Children And Youth With Disabilities

The changes we need aren't just about providing better services but about making fundamental shifts in how we design our communities, organizations, and societies. One such shift is the understanding of universal design, which suggests that we should create environments, products, and services that are accessible to everyone from the very beginning, rather than retrofitting accommodations later.

When I visit schools that have been designed with universal design principles, I see wide hallways that accommodate wheelchairs but also make it easier for everyone to move around. I see classrooms with excellent acoustics that help children with hearing impairments but also create better learning environments for all students. I see flexible seating options that support children with ADHD while giving every student choices about how they learn best.

The same principles apply to digital accessibility. Websites and apps designed with screen readers in mind often turn out to be easier for everyone to navigate. Captions on videos help people who are deaf or have difficulties with hearing, but they also help people learning a new language or watching in noisy environments.

I encourage every organization I work with to think about accessibility from the planning stage, not as an afterthought. This means consulting with people with disabilities during the design process, conducting accessibility audits, and viewing accommodation not as a burden but as an opportunity to create better solutions for everyone.

We must also understand that creating truly inclusive environments requires more than just physical accessibility, but a great deal of cultural transformation. I have seen organizations that have all the right policies on paper but still exclude people with disabilities through subtle biases, low expectations, or failure to truly include diverse perspectives in decision-making.

The organizations that succeed in creating inclusive cultures are those that actively recruit people with disabilities not just as clients or beneficiaries, but as staff members, board members, and leaders. They provide ongoing training about disability awareness and inclusion. They regularly assess their practices for barriers and are willing to change long-standing procedures when they create exclusion.

These organizations also understand that inclusion benefits everyone. When they create flexible work policies to accommodate employees with disabilities, they often find that all employees appreciate the flexibility. When they improve their communication methods to be more accessible, they discover that everyone communicates more effectively.

In the aspect of education, beyond having separate special education systems, we must fundamentally reimagine how we teach all children. I am particularly excited to see developments in personalized learning technologies, multi-sensory teaching methods, and collaborative learning approaches that benefit everyone.

Going forward, I am sure we all want to see classrooms where students with and without disabilities work together on projects, where assistive technology is seamlessly integrated, and where different learning styles are celebrated rather than merely tolerated. In these environments, children with disabilities won't be seen as needing special help, but recognized as bringing different perspectives and strengths to the learning community. Teacher preparation programs should also include training in inclusive education, disability awareness, and universal design for learning.

Technology also has its role to play here. We need to see more communication apps that will give voices to children who previously couldn't express themselves, smart home technologies that allow young people with physical disabilities to control their environments independently, and virtual reality devices that provide safe spaces to practice social skills and mobility techniques.

But then, I also recognize the fact that technology is only as good as its accessibility and affordability; therefore, I advocate to ensure that assistive technologies are covered by insurance, that mainstream technologies are designed with accessibility in mind, and that families have support in learning to use new tools effectively (for the benefit of their wards with disabilities).

The future requires us to think beyond specialized disability services toward creating communities where everyone belongs naturally. This would mean accessible public transportation, inclusive recreation programs, job opportunities that value diverse abilities, and social environments where disability is seen as one form of human diversity rather than something to be hidden or overcome. In light of this, communities must conduct accessibility audits not just of their buildings but also of their programs, events, and social activities.

Finally, we must begin to see more strategic policy changes in healthcare, education, and work settings that address systemic barriers and discrimination. I advocate for robust enforcement of disability rights laws, increased funding for accessible education and community services, and policies that support families caring for children with disabilities. By doing this, real opportunities for people with disabilities to contribute their talents will be created.

Reflections and Conclusion

If you are reading this as a parent or caregiver of a child with a disability, I want you to know that your love, advocacy, and daily commitment make an enormous difference. I have worked with families long enough and have watched them navigate complex systems, fight for their children's rights, and celebrate achievements that others might take for granted. Your dedication is heroic, and I greatly commend your efforts.

Please remember that you don't have to be perfect. You don't have to know everything or have all the answers. What matters is that you keep showing up, keep learning, and keep believing in your child's potential. Seek out other families who share similar experiences, as their wisdom and support can be invaluable.

Remember also that taking care of yourself is essential. You cannot pour from an empty cup. Find respite when you need it, celebrate small victories, and don't let anyone diminish your child's worth or your family's dreams.

For professionals in the healthcare system, your words and attitudes have profound power. When you receive a family with a child who has just been diagnosed with a disability, you're not just sharing medical information but shaping how that family will understand their child's life and potential. Lead with hope while being honest about challenges. Help families understand their child's condition without defining the child by that condition. Connect families with resources and support networks, and remember that healing encompasses much more than medical intervention.

Consider how your clinical environment feels to children with disabilities and their families. Is it welcoming? Is it accessible? Do your communication methods accommodate different needs? Are you working with families as partners rather than simply delivering services to them?

Educators, you have the extraordinary opportunity to influence how an entire generation understands disability and inclusion. When you create classrooms where every child belongs, where differences are celebrated, and where high expectations exist for all students, you are not just teaching academic content; you are teaching humanity. Every time you adapt your teaching methods to reach a child with different learning needs, you become a better teacher for all your students. Every time you facilitate friendships between children with and without disabilities, you're building a more inclusive future. Every time you see potential rather than limitations, you change a life.

Please advocate within your systems for the resources and training you need to serve all children effectively, push back against low expectations, and collaborate with families as true partners.

To the social workers (of which I am one), your role as advocates and connectors is vital in the healing process. Help families understand that needing support isn't a sign of weakness but a part of the human experience. Connect them not just with services, but with communities where they can find understanding and belonging. Advocate for policies and practices that truly serve families rather than creating additional barriers. Also, remember that families are the experts on their own children. Your role is to support their goals and dreams, not to impose your own vision of what their lives should look like.

Finally, and most importantly, I want to speak directly to the young people living with disabilities who are reading these words. Your experiences, your dreams, and your voices matter more than anything else in this conversation about healing and inclusion.

I want you to hear clearly what Crystal Asige discovered in her journey: you may not be able to change your circumstances, but you have the power to change how you look at your circumstances. This isn't about denying real challenges or pretending that discrimination doesn't exist. It's about recognizing that your worth, your potential, and your future aren't defined by other people's limitations or prejudices.

I know there are voices in your head, maybe voices from society, from well-meaning but misguided people, or even from your own fears, that tell you that you're less than, that you should be grateful for whatever crumbs of acceptance you receive, that you should make yourself smaller to make others comfortable. I am here to tell you to turn down the volume on those voices until they become whispers, and then silence them altogether.

You have every right to take up space in this world. You have every right to dream big dreams and pursue them relentlessly. You have every right to expect that the world will adapt to include you, rather than requiring you to change yourself to fit into spaces that were poorly designed in the first place.

Your disability is part of your story, but it's not the whole story. You are not defined by what you cannot do; you are defined by who you choose to become. And who you choose to become should be the most authentic, bold, unapologetic version of yourself that you can imagine. Don't let anyone convince you to settle for less than you deserve. Don't let anyone tell you that asking for accessibility, accommodation, or inclusion is asking for too much. Don't let anyone make you feel like you should be grateful for basic human dignity and respect.

At the same time, don't stop growing. Don't stop learning. Don't stop developing your talents and skills. The world needs what you have to offer, but you need to be prepared to offer it boldly and excellently. Become so skilled, so knowledgeable, and so valuable in your chosen areas that people can't ignore your contributions.

Build connections with other people with disabilities who can serve as mentors, friends, and collaborators. Advocate for yourself and for others. Use your voice to point out barriers, suggest solutions, and demand change. The world needs your perspective, your creativity, and your leadership. Don't wait for someone else to speak for you. Speak for yourself, and speak loudly enough that you cannot be ignored.

Remember that healing isn't about becoming "normal" or fitting into someone else's definition of acceptable. Healing is about becoming whole—integrating all parts of yourself, finding peace with your reality while still working toward your dreams, and discovering the unique purpose that only you can fulfil.

As Crystal Asige said in her powerful testimony, "I have glaucoma, but glaucoma does not have me." Whatever your disability might be, never forget: you have a disability, but your disability does not have you. You are the author of your own story, the architect of your own dreams, and the agent of your own future.

Rise up. Speak out. Take your place. The world is waiting for what only you can give.

CHAPTER EIGHT
HEALING FOR CHILDREN & YOUTH IN FOSTER CARE SYSTEMS

The foster care system was designed to be a temporary safe haven for children who can't live with their biological families due to abuse, neglect, or other serious family problems. The main objective of the foster care system is to provide these children with stable, nurturing care while working toward either reunifying them with their families or matching them with permanent adoptive homes.

Children enrolled on the foster care system have already experienced significant trauma and loss. They have been migrated from the known to the unknown, and even when such migration or removal was necessary for their safety, it represents another phase of loss in young lives that have often already experienced significant loss.

Before we dive deeper into healing approaches, it is crucial to understand why children enter foster care systems in the first place. The reasons are complex and often interconnected, ranging from individual family crises to systemic societal failures.

Why Foster Care?

I have worked and interacted with foster youths, and I have so far learned that behind every placement decision lies a story of profound loss. Children do not enter foster care because their parents are inherently bad people; they enter because families have reached breaking points where they can no longer provide safe, stable care. This might be due to untreated mental illness, substance abuse, domestic violence, extreme poverty, or the absence of adequate social supports.

The trauma that brings children into care is often compounded by the trauma of separation itself. Picture being removed from everything that makes sense to you, like your home, your school, your neighborhood, your siblings, and all you can think of, and being placed with strangers. No matter how well-intentioned they might be, you will definitely feel the impact of that separation.

For many children, this represents a second layer of trauma on top of whatever circumstances necessitated their removal.

In Africa, Nigeria specifically, the reasons children end up in institutional care are similarly complex but often tied to broader structural issues. The Association of Orphanages and Home Operators in Nigeria (ASOHON) has called for urgent steps to strengthen Nigeria's foster care system as a sustainable alternative for the care and protection of vulnerable children. Many children in Nigerian orphanages aren't truly orphans, but children whose families couldn't afford to care for them, or who were abandoned due to disability, illness, or social stigma.

For Canada and the United States, the Human Rights Watch & American Civil Liberties Union posit that poverty, rather than abuse, is often the primary factor in child welfare involvement. Families struggling with housing instability, food insecurity, or lack of access to mental health services are more likely to come to the attention of child protection services. This raises critical questions about whether we're addressing root causes or simply responding to symptoms.

Let us narrow the searchlight on Canada, where I live and work.
Over here, foster care can take many forms, ranging from private foster homes to institutionalized group homes. In contrast, in many African countries (specifically in Nigeria), the concept of formal foster care is largely non-existent. There, children and youth without family support are typically placed in orphanages or live under the care of trusted relatives, church leaders, or compassionate community members.

One of the key distinctions is that in Canada and other Western countries, foster caregivers are financially compensated by the government. This is part of a well-structured system supported by funding, policies, and awareness. In Nigeria, foster care is more often driven by communal responsibility or religious obligation, with little to no financial support for caregivers. However, this isn't to say one approach is more noble than the other, as compassion exists in both systems. Having worked in a foster group home in Canada myself, I know firsthand the emotional commitment required in this field.

Although financial compensation is part of the Canadian system, many foster workers are underpaid, especially considering the emotional, physical, and psychological labor involved. The child and youth care sector remains one of the most undervalued in terms of pay despite its crucial societal role.

The number of youths in the Canadian foster care system is high, with statistics showing overrepresentation of certain racial and cultural groups. Meanwhile, in countries like Nigeria, these youth may exist but are often not recognized within an official system due to the absence of such frameworks. This leads to different forms of resilience and survival strategies among youth in those environments.

There is immense strength in young people who emerge from these structures and go on to shape better futures for themselves, and even advocate for systemic reform. However, to discuss the foster system without examining its policies would be incomplete.

In Canada, for example, certain policies may be culturally misaligned or insufficient to address the unique needs of racialized or marginalized youths.

The lived experiences of youth in care vary widely. Some have relatively mild experiences, while others endure severe trauma. Every interaction with staff, social workers, peers, and institutions, shape their reality. Healing in this context must be approached as a deeply personal, individualized journey. No two youth heal the same way. One person's turning point may differ completely from another's.

Let's take a deep look at the Canadian foster care system before examining its counterpart in Nigeria. In Canada, group homes (especially institutional ones) are often associated with mixed feelings.

From my experience working in a group home, I remember both sweet and bitter moments. A common sentiment among youth in care is suspicion towards the workers: "You're only here for the money; no one really cares about me." These feelings are valid and must be acknowledged.

Research available from the National Foster Youth Institute shows that institutionalized youths in care frequently encounter racism, bias, and systemic discrimination—whether in education, healthcare, or legal systems. Society often imposes a stigma on these children, placing them in metaphorical boxes and limiting their perceived potential.

One of the key roles of a foster worker is to see beyond the files and diagnoses, and see the child or youth as a person. Many of these youth carry trauma from past violence, neglect, abuse, family separation, or loss of identity. These, and more, make their stories layered and complex. Let's take Sara, for example:

(Sara's Story)

Sara was a friendly and intelligent young woman, but she displayed aggressive behaviors, especially towards staff and authority figures. According to her file, she had experienced childhood sexual abuse from a relative after immigrating to Canada. Her parents had passed away early in her life, and she had no siblings or close family support. Years of carrying unspoken pain, stigma, and shame had built up into explosive anger.

Sara had multiple assault charges, not against peers, but against staff. These actions, while difficult to manage, were rooted in unresolved trauma. With time, a strong support system, and the application of a strength-based approach which focuses on the youth's potential and abilities rather than deficits, we saw real progress. Sara began to stabilize, and eventually transitioned into independent living. She later returned to the organization as a peer mentor, supporting youth in situations she once lived through.

Then there's Kyle.

(Kyle's Story)

Kyle was placed in a transitional group home, typically a short-term stay for assessment and placement. However, due to systemic delays, he remained there for over a year. Kyle struggled with the legal system, substance use, and violent behavior, including a serious incident in his community.

He had cycled through several social workers, but his case shows how gaps in the system (particularly around placement delays and trauma-informed care) can impact youth outcomes.

Indigenous View On Healing

Indigenous approaches to healing for foster youths are focused on reconnection—to culture, to land, to community, and to spiritual traditions. Traditional indigenous cultures contain the strengths that create the capacity to cope effectively with crisis and trauma, even in contexts like this. The Indigenous Healing and Seeking Safety intervention was adapted to include sessions targeted at historical trauma and historical loss symptoms. The adapted intervention emphasized elements of the medicine wheel and taught traditional activities to foster sobriety and heal trauma.

Many Indigenous youth in care have been disconnected from their cultural heritage. Healing involves reclaiming traditional knowledge, language, and practices. This might include participating in sweat lodge ceremonies, learning traditional crafts, or connecting with elders who can share cultural wisdom.

Indigenous healing approaches explicitly address how historical trauma, from residential schools, forced removals, and cultural genocide, continues to impact families and communities. Youths learn that their family's struggles are not personal failures but consequences of systematic oppression.

Rather than individual therapy sessions, Indigenous healing often happens in community settings, talking circles, community feasts, and ceremonial gatherings where youth experience belonging and collective support.

Let us not also forget that the success of Indigenous healing approaches offers important lessons for all foster care systems: the importance of cultural connection, community support, and addressing root causes of trauma rather than just symptoms.

Western View On Healing

Western approaches to healing foster youth typically center on evidence-based clinical interventions, individual therapy, and symptom management. These approaches have evolved significantly over recent decades, with increasing recognition of trauma's impact on development and behavior.

To illustrate the lived experience that often necessitates Western therapeutic interventions, I want to share a powerful testimony from someone who survived the foster care system. This account comes from a young person who spent 13 years in care across 60+ placements:

"I was in Foster Care from 2005-2018. I was in over 60+ Placements During that time. It was the Worst Experience to ever happen to me.

I entered foster care at the tender age of 5 years old with 2 older siblings who had been taken at the same time due to abuse, neglect, and lack of proper food. When we were taken, we were separated pretty much immediately. I can still hear the wailing and feel the devastation I had as we were put in the car and dropped off one by one, saying our goodbyes to each other. I was the last one to be dropped off.

I remember going to placements that had dusty bars and tinted glass on the windows, limited free time, and 1 hour per day outdoor time. Cameras everywhere. It didn't help that I have a mental disability, so I was a target for being not only bullied at school, but at home where the adults in charge of me picked favorites and taunted me.

All doors were locked at some of the placements. Donations given by gracious donors, such as toys and electronics, were taken from me and sold. I wasn't allowed to call or write letters to my siblings due to us 'misbehaving' at the separate placements we were at.

Being thrown out in the snow in freezing temperatures in nothing but a tank top and tiny shorts at 12 years old. Constant threats of the cops being called because I wasn't acting happy or smiling. Being forced to walk over 2 miles to school while a perfectly good car was being driven next to me, the adult inside was taunting me and laughing.

Constant bullying and racism from adults and others in the home. Being slammed and thrown against walls for having an attitude and being screamed at. I remember my vision going black and seeing stars.

I remember my eyes being swollen shut when I woke up one morning due to allergies, barely able to breathe, calling out for help but being told to stop being dramatic and that I was faking it. I had to crawl to the living room, wheezing for air, just to be laughed at.

Forced to sleep outside as a little kid, locked outside and taunted when a wild coyote was approaching me, growling. Being made fun of for the way I look by adults. Not being allowed to speak of things going on, due to threat of punishment.

Constantly getting jumped by older kids as the adults just watched for entertainment. Having gifts and clothes constantly taken from me and given to others or sold by the adults for their own gain. Being denied new things while watching other kids in the home get what they wanted.

Never taken to the doctor and told to suck it up, even when I was bleeding and crying. Forced to do manual labor for pennies while suffering from severe allergies.

I was talked out of being adopted multiple times because I was 'too angry' and nobody would want me, and they would just send me back.

I left the system at 18 and moved to other placements that were supposed to help me, too, but that's another story.

I am doing a bit better now; I decided to go to therapy and get on meds for my mental disability. Met the love of my life, who supports me through this all, so that's great."

This testimony illustrates the complex trauma that Western therapeutic approaches attempt to address. The experiences described—multiple placements, institutional abuse, separation from siblings, racial discrimination, medical neglect, and psychological abuse—create layered trauma that requires comprehensive clinical intervention.

Key Western Therapeutic Approaches for Foster Youth

Trauma-Informed Care: Modern Western approaches recognize that most foster youths have experienced significant trauma. Treatment focuses on understanding how trauma affects brain development, behavior, and relationships. Therapeutic interventions help youth process traumatic experiences and develop healthy coping mechanisms.

Attachment Theory and Therapy: Foster youths often struggle with attachment due to early disruptions in primary relationships. Attachment-based therapies help youth understand their relationship patterns and develop secure attachments with caregivers and peers.

Cognitive-Behavioral Therapy (CBT): CBT helps youths identify and change negative thought patterns and behaviors that developed as survival mechanisms, but may no longer serve them. This approach is particularly effective for addressing anxiety, depression, and behavioral challenges.

Dialectical Behavior Therapy (DBT): Originally developed for individuals with borderline personality disorder, DBT has proven effective for foster youths who struggle with emotional regulation, self-harm, and interpersonal difficulties.

Medication Management: Some foster youths benefit from psychiatric medications to address conditions like ADHD, depression, or anxiety. Western approaches emphasize careful monitoring and collaboration between medical professionals, therapists, and caregivers.

Individual and Group Therapy: Both individual and group therapy settings offer unique benefits. Individual therapy allows for processing personal trauma, while group therapy provides peer support and reduces isolation.

Family Therapy: When appropriate, family therapy can help biological families address issues that led to placement and work toward reunification. For youth aging out of care, therapy might focus on building chosen family relationships.

The young person's story above illustrates both the need for these interventions and their potential effectiveness. Despite experiencing severe trauma and abuse within the system, they found healing through therapy, medication, and supportive relationships. Their journey demonstrates that recovery is possible even after profound trauma.

Afrocentric View On Healing

Afrocentric approaches to healing for children and youths in the foster system, emphasizes community connection, cultural pride, and collective healing. These approaches recognize that individual healing cannot be separated from community wellness and cultural restoration.

An Afrocentric approach to Black health promotes culturally meaningful health care grounded in the values, worldviews, lived experiences and histories of Black people of African descent. This philosophy extends naturally to working with foster youth, many of whom have been disconnected not only from their families but from their cultural communities.

Dr. Hassan, an Afrocentric therapist working with Black foster youths, once mentioned that when African-descended children enter care, they often lose connection to their cultural identity, their community, and their understanding of their place in the world. Healing requires more than addressing individual symptoms. it also requires cultural restoration and community reconnection.

Core Principles of Afrocentric Healing for Foster Youths

Ubuntu Philosophy: In Ubuntu, children are seen as active contributors and agents of change and communal healing. This principle recognizes that children are not passive recipients of care but active participants in their own healing and the healing of their communities.

Foster youths are supported to understand their interconnectedness with their community and their potential to contribute positively to collective wellness. This stands in contrast to deficit-based approaches that view foster youth primarily through the lens of their problems or pathology.

Cultural Affirmation and Identity Development: Many Black foster youths have internalized negative messages about their identity, their families, and their communities. Afrocentric healing actively counters these messages through cultural education, pride development, and positive identity formation.

This might involve learning African history and contributions, participating in cultural celebrations, connecting with positive Black role models, and developing critical consciousness about racism and oppression.

Collective Healing Approaches: NTU psychotherapy is based on the core principles of the ancient African and Afrocentric worldview, nurtured through African American culture. NTU therapy and other Afrocentric therapeutic approaches emphasize that healing happens in the community rather than in isolation.

Group healing circles, mentorship programs, and community-based interventions show that healing is enhanced when it happens in connection with others who share similar experiences and cultural backgrounds.

Spiritual and Ancestral Connection: Afrocentric approaches often incorporate spiritual dimensions of healing, including connection to ancestors and spiritual practices rooted in African traditions. For foster youths who may feel disconnected from their roots, these practices can provide grounding and meaning.

Addressing Systemic Oppression: Afrocentric healing explicitly addresses how racism and systemic oppression contribute to the challenges faced by Black families and communities. Youth learn to understand their experiences within broader social and historical contexts, reducing self-blame and shame.

Rites of Passage and Community Celebration: Traditional African cultures mark important life transitions with community ceremonies and rites of passage. Afrocentric programs for foster youth often incorporate these elements, celebrating achievements, marking milestones, and providing community recognition of the youth's growth and contributions.

Dr. Hassan shared the story of Marcus, a 17-year-old who had been in care since age 12. Through an Afrocentric mentorship program, Marcus connected with a Black male mentor who introduced him to African history, participated in rites of passage ceremonies, and helped him develop leadership skills through community service.

"Marcus went from seeing himself as a 'problem kid' to understanding himself as a young African king with tremendous potential," Dr. Hassan explained. *"The transformation wasn't just individual, because as Marcus healed, he began mentoring younger children in the program."*

Effective Afrocentric healing programs often merge cultural and clinical approaches, educational support, and practical life skills development. The Dandelion Philosophy's concept of Afrocentric psychology provides a culturally sensitive approach to healing intergenerational trauma. This approach emphasizes the unique strengths and challenges of being black or brown, as well as providing hope and positive change within our communities.

One major challenge facing Afrocentric approaches is the lack of funding and institutional support for culturally specific programming.

Many mainstream foster care systems don't recognize or fund cultural healing approaches, despite evidence of their effectiveness.

However, there's growing recognition of the importance of cultural approaches. The Family Navigation Project (FNP) at Sunnybrook is a Mental Health and Addictions Navigation Service for youth ages 11-29 within the Greater Toronto Area (GTA) that has begun integrating Afrocentric approaches into its service delivery model.

Christocentric Views On Healing

Christian approaches to healing for foster youths are centered on spiritual transformation, faith community support, and understanding of God's love and purpose for each child. These approaches are particularly significant in many foster care contexts, as faith-based organizations operate a substantial portion of foster care services globally.

In Nigeria, for instance, many foster homes are affiliated with Christian religious denominations, and they work together to groom and cater to the needs of children and youth in those facilities.

Speaking during a session at a faith-based residential program for foster youth in Nigeria, a renowned pastor and founder of the home mentioned that when children have been hurt and abandoned, our role is to reflect God's unconditional love and help them understand their identity as beloved children of God.

Core Elements of Christian Healing for Foster Youth

Identity in Christ: Christian approaches emphasize helping youth understand their identity as beloved children of God, regardless of their past experiences or current circumstances. This provides a foundation of worth and purpose that transcends trauma and rejection.

For foster youth who have often experienced rejection and abandonment, the message of God's unconditional love can be profoundly healing. Youth learn that their value doesn't depend on their behavior, their family background, or their achievements, but on their inherent worth as God's children.

Prayer and Spiritual Practices: Christian healing approaches incorporate prayer, worship, scripture study, and other spiritual disciplines as therapeutic interventions. These practices provide comfort, hope, and connection to the divine during difficult times.

A young man who aged out of care in Alabama once described how prayer helped him cope with the isolation and fear of independent living. According to him, when he felt completely alone and scared about his future, prayer reminded him that God was with him. That gave him the strength to keep going when everything felt hopeless."

Faith Community Support: Christian approaches emphasize the role of faith communities in providing support, mentorship, and belonging for foster youths. Churches, youth groups, and faith-based mentorship programs create extended family networks for youths who lack biological family support.

These communities often provide practical support, including help with housing, employment, education funding, life skills, alongside spiritual and emotional support. The combination of practical and spiritual care addresses multiple dimensions of the youth's needs.

Forgiveness and Redemption: Christian healing emphasizes the possibility of forgiveness and redemption, both receiving forgiveness and extending it to others. For foster youth who may carry guilt, shame, or anger related to their experiences, the message of God's forgiveness can be liberating. This doesn't mean minimizing trauma or excusing abuse, but rather providing a path toward freedom from the psychological burden of unforgiveness and self-blame.

Purpose and Calling: Christian approaches help youth identify their gifts, talents, and calling from God. Many foster youth struggle with feelings of worthlessness or a lack of direction. Discovering their God-given purpose can provide motivation and hope for the future.

Biblical Models of Restoration: Christian teaching provides numerous examples of individuals who overcame difficult circumstances through faith—from Joseph's journey from slavery to leadership, to David's transformation from shepherd to king. These stories provide hope and models for resilience.

***

However, Christian approaches to foster care healing has face several challenges,, including but not limited to:

Religious diversity: Foster youths come from diverse religious backgrounds, and imposing Christian beliefs can be harmful rather than healing

Quality control: Not all faith-based programs maintain high standards of care or evidence-based practices

Separation of church and state: In publicly-funded systems, there are legal and ethical constraints on religious programming

Trauma-informed practice: Some faith-based approaches may inadvertently blame victims or minimize trauma

The most effective Christian approaches are those that respect religious diversity, maintain high professional standards, integrate evidence-based practices, and provide genuine unconditional love and support regardless of youth's response to religious messages. Similarly, many effective programs involve collaboration between Christian organizations and other faith communities, recognizing that spiritual healing can take many forms depending on the youth's background and beliefs.

The Way Forward for Children and Youth in Foster Homes

When I think about the thousands of children and young people living in foster care systems around the world, my heart breaks but also swells with hope. These are kids who have experienced loss in its most profound forms–separation from biological families, disrupted attachments, and often multiple placements that can feel like a series of fresh wounds just as the old ones begin to heal.

But then, these incredible young souls possess the kind of resilience that would humble most adults. They've survived things that would break many of us, and yet they continue to hope, to dream, to reach out for connection even when every experience has taught them that people leave.

The way forward for these children isn't about erasing their past or pretending their losses don't matter. It's about helping them understand their story. All of it, including the painful chapters that shaped them into survivors with unique strengths.

For teenagers in care, the path forward often involves helping them reclaim their true selves. These young people have frequently been defined by their circumstances – the "foster kid," the "troubled teen," and the "system child." But they are so much more than their placement status. They are artists, athletes, dreamers, and leaders. They are young people with opinions, talents, and contributions to make to the world.

The way forward also means preparing them for independence without rushing them towards it. Many youths in care face the terrifying prospect of aging out of the system, often without the family safety net that most young adults take for granted. They need practical skills, yes, but they also need emotional preparation for managing grief and loss as independent adults.

Most importantly, the way forward involves helping these young people understand that their ability to form healthy relationships is not broken, but just interrupted. With patience, consistency, and genuine care, they can learn to trust again, love again, and build the families they choose, even if they're different from the families they were born into.

Reflections and Conclusion

If you are a social worker reading this, I want you to know something: you are doing holy work. Every day, you step into the messiest, most heartbreaking, and most complicated situations imaginable, and you show up anyway. You advocate for children who can't advocate for themselves. You sit in court hearings that determine the trajectory of young lives. You make impossible decisions with incomplete information and then live with the weight of those choices.

I know there are days when you wonder if anything you do makes a difference. I know you've lost sleep worrying about a child on your caseload. I know you've felt the system fail despite your best efforts, and I know you've carried guilt that isn't yours to carry.

But please hear this: you matter more than you know. That child who couldn't look you in the eye during your first meeting but now runs to hug you? That teenager who was convinced all adults would eventually abandon them but now texts you about college plans? That sibling group that stayed together because you fought for them? These aren't small things. These are miracles dressed up as ordinary moments.

To the foster parents, kinship caregivers, and residential care staff who provide daily care for these children: you are not just providing shelter and meals. You are providing something far more precious – the experience of being valued, of mattering to someone, of having adults who show up consistently even when things get hard.

Some of the children in your care will test every boundary you set, not because they don't want your love, but because they need to know if your love is conditional. Some will seem ungrateful for your efforts, not because they don't appreciate what you're doing, but because gratitude requires vulnerability, and vulnerability has been dangerous for them in the past.

Your patience in those moments, your consistency when they expect abandonment, and your gentle persistence when they push you away—these acts of love are rewriting their understanding of what relationships can be. You are literally rewiring their brains for trust, teaching them through your actions that not all adults leave, that safety can be real, that they are worthy of care.

And to the young people who are living this experience—whether you're currently in care, have aged out, or are somewhere in between—I want you to know that your story is not finished. The chapters that brought you into care, as painful as they may have been, are not the end of your book. They are not even the most important chapters, though they may feel that way right now.

You have survived 100% of your worst days. Think about that for a moment. Every loss, every placement change, every disappointment, every moment when you thought you couldn't go on—you survived all of it. That is not luck but a display of strength and resilience. That's proof that you have something unbreakable inside you.

Your grief is valid. Your anger is understandable. Your fear of getting too attached makes perfect sense. But please don't let these natural responses to unnatural circumstances convince you that you're broken or that you don't deserve love. You deserve all the love in the world, and more importantly, you have the capacity to give and receive it, even if it doesn't feel that way right now.

As you move forward, whether you're planning for independence or working on healing old wounds, remember that seeking help isn't weakness but wisdom. The strongest people I know are the ones who've learned to reach out when they need support. Don't try to carry everything alone.

Your past has prepared you for a future that only you can create. You get to decide what kind of adult you become, what kind of relationships you build, and what kind of family you create or join. The little child inside you who experienced those early losses deserves to see you thrive, to see you happy, and to see you loved.

The journey truly isn't over. In many ways, it's just beginning.

CHAPTER NINE
HEALING FOR MIGRANT AND DISPLACED CHILDREN & YOUTH

I recall when I first stepped off the plane in a country that wasn't home, clutching my passport and carrying dreams wrapped in uncertainty. That moment, suspended between who I had been and who I might become, painted a fine picture of resilience, which is required when home becomes a memory.

Now, years later, as I work with migrant and displaced children and youths across different continents, I understand that my experience was just a drop in the ocean of human movement. Some stories tell of choice and opportunity, while others tell of urgency and survival. Each of them, however, carries the weight of transformation, loss, and the remarkable capacity of young people to adapt, heal, and thrive against all odds.

Migrant youths are those who move from place to place with some degree of choice and planning, and they carry their own unique set of experiences and needs.

In my work with this population, I have realized that voluntary movement doesn't necessarily mean movement without difficulty. The fifteen-year-old who joins her parents seeking better educational opportunities faces cultural adaptation challenges. The eighteen-year-old pursuing university education abroad grapples with homesickness and identity questions. The young person reuniting with family members experiences the complexity of changed relationships across time and distance.

The resilience I observe in migrant youth often comes from their sense of agency in the movement process. Even when the decision wasn't entirely their own, they often understand the reasoning behind it and can construct narratives that frame their migration as an opportunity, rather than a loss. This doesn't eliminate challenges, but it provides a different foundation for adaptation and healing.

Displaced youths, by contrast, have experienced movement characterized by urgency, fear, and often trauma. Their journeys begin not with planning and hope, but with threat and necessity. In my conversations with displaced young people, I have heard different stories, and most of them were marked by sudden separation, dangerous journeys, and the ongoing uncertainty that comes with seeking safety.

The trauma that often accompanies displacement creates additional layers of complexity. Unlike migrant youth who might struggle with cultural adaptation but maintain psychological safety, displaced youth often heal from trauma while simultaneously navigating new environments. This dual process requires specialized support that addresses both psychological wounds and practical adaptation needs.

From my observation, displaced youths often demonstrate incredible survival skills and protective instincts, particularly those who become separated from families or take on caregiving roles for younger siblings. However, these premature responsibilities can also complicate their healing processes.

In reality, the difference between migrant and displaced youth isn't always clear-cut. Climate change creates situations where families migrate preventively but also flee sudden disasters. Economic desperation can make migration feel less voluntary. Political instability can transform a planned movement into an urgent flight.

I remember a youth who left Honduras at fifteen. His family initially planned to migrate for economic opportunities, but escalating gang violence made their departure urgent and dangerous. "We thought we were moving for my father's new job," he explained, "but by the time we left, we were running for our lives." This is one out of many experiences that should remind us that young people's relationships with movement can sometimes be complex and unpredictable.

This intersection matters for healing work because it shapes how young people understand their experiences and construct their identities. Those who can frame their movement as choice often develop different coping strategies than those who experience it as forced. However, both groups may benefit from interventions that acknowledge the complexity of their experiences and avoid rigid categorizations.

For young people, migration rarely happens in isolation. So let's pop the question: Why do young people migrate?

Why Youths Migrate

Educational Aspirations and Opportunities:

One of the most powerful drivers of youth migration is education. I've worked with countless young people who cross borders pursuing academic opportunities unavailable in their home countries. Many of these youths are supported by their entire extended family's savings, and this reflects how millions of young people worldwide see education as a pathway to better futures, not just for themselves, but for their families and communities.

Educational migration often comes with unique psychological challenges. These young people carry intense pressure to succeed, knowing that their families have invested significant resources in their opportunities. The twenty-three-year-old medical student from Nigeria studying in Ukraine before the war, the seventeen-year-old from Guatemala pursuing high school completion in the United States, the twenty-year-old from rural China attending university in Australia, all carry dreams that extend far beyond individual achievement.

One thing I love about these educationally motivated young migrants is their long-term thinking and goal orientation. They often demonstrate remarkable perseverance through cultural and linguistic challenges because they maintain clear visions of their desired futures. However, this future focus can sometimes make them vulnerable to isolation and stress when progress feels slow or obstacles seem insurmountable.

Economic Necessity and Family Survival:

Economic factors drive migration for many young people, either as primary migrants seeking work opportunities or as family members in household economic strategies. In my work, I've met teenagers who migrate to send remittances home, young adults who join family businesses in destination countries, and youth who pursue migration as the only viable alternative to poverty.

Economic migration among youth often involves significant sacrifice and responsibility. Eighteen-year-old Rosa left Mexico to work in agricultural fields in California, sending most of her earnings home to support her younger siblings' education. Her migration story is simultaneously one of economic opportunity and family devotion, reflecting how young people often carry adult responsibilities while still developing their own identities.

The psychological impact of economically motivated migration can be complex. Young people may experience pride in their ability to support their families alongside grief for delayed personal dreams. They may develop strong work ethics and practical skills while missing educational or social opportunities typical for their age group. Supporting these young migrants requires understanding their dual roles as both youth in development and economic contributors to family survival.

Family Reunification and Social Networks:

Many young migrants move to reunite with family members who migrated earlier, joining established diaspora communities that provide both support and expectations. These reunification migrations often involve complex emotional dynamics like joy at family reunion, combined with adjustment challenges in relationships that have evolved during separation.

Social networks play crucial roles in youth migration, providing information, resources, and community connections that facilitate movement and adaptation. However, these networks can also create pressures and expectations that complicate young people's experiences.

The Ghanaian teenager joining an established community in New York may benefit from cultural familiarity while feeling constrained by community expectations about behavior and achievement.

Adventure, Independence, and Self-Discovery

Some young people migrate driven by desires for adventure, independence, and self-discovery. These motivations, while sometimes dismissed as privilege, reflect important developmental needs for autonomy and identity exploration. I've worked with young people who participated in exchange programs, pursued working holidays, or sought life experiences unavailable in their home countries.

While these migrants often have more resources and support systems, they still face adaptation challenges and identity questions.

When we understand these diverse migration motivations, we would be able to recognize that young migrants aren't a homogeneous group requiring identical support. Educational migrants may need academic support and career guidance. Economically motivated migrants may need labor rights education and financial literacy. Family reunification migrants may need relationship counseling and cultural mediation. Adventure-seeking migrants may need independence development and decision-making support.

Factors Driving Youth Displacement

Before exploring the specific factors that force young people from their homes, it's essential to reiterate how displacement differs fundamentally from migration. While migration involves some degree of choice and planning—even if those choices are constrained by economic or social factors—displacement represents involuntary movement driven by immediate threats to safety and survival.

According to the International Organization for Migration, forced migration involves "force, compulsion, or coercion," while voluntary migration follows economic cost-benefit considerations of the migrants. However, in practice, many movements exist along a spectrum between purely voluntary and completely forced.

When I work with young people, I learn to listen to how they describe their movement experiences rather than imposing categories upon them. The UNHCR defines forced displacement as movement "as a result of persecution, conflict, generalized violence or human rights violations", but young people's lived experiences often involve multiple, overlapping factors that don't fit neatly into policy definitions.

What then are these factors? Let's consider a number of them.

Armed Conflict and Violence:

According to the United Nations High Commissioner for Refugees, armed conflict remains one of the most devastating drivers of youth displacement. Globally, there has been an estimated 230 percent increase in the number of forcibly displaced children both within countries and across borders as a result of persecution, conflict, generalized violence, human rights violations, or events seriously disturbing public order.

In my work with conflict-displaced youth, I've learned that violence affects them in ways that extend far beyond immediate physical threats. Young people displaced by conflict often witness community destruction, experience family separation, endure dangerous journeys, and face ongoing uncertainty about return possibilities. These experiences shape not only their immediate needs but also their long-term development and worldview.

Let us consider Ukraine as a case study.

The scale of Ukrainian displacement during periods of conflict is usually staggering. More than 6 million people have fled Ukraine, mostly women and children, while 8 million remain displaced inside the country. In Save the Children's latest needs assessment, 85% of families reported needing psychosocial support, with heartbreaking accounts of children unable to sleep, constantly afraid, crying, and refusing to leave bomb shelters.

What I've observed from my research on Ukrainian children is that their trauma manifests in layers. There's the acute trauma of witnessing violence, the ongoing stress of uncertainty, and the complex grief of losing not just a home but an entire way of life. Programs like Parent-Child Care (PC-CARE), designed to help families strengthen bonds and manage trauma-induced stress, have emerged as promising interventions, trained by institutions like the University of California Davis and adapted for Ukrainian families.

One of the most pressing concerns for Ukrainian refugee children is education access, specifically early learning and secondary education, alongside child protection and cross-border support. So far, there have been remarkable adaptations in host countries. These include online Ukrainian schools continuing curriculum delivery, bilingual programs emerging in Poland and Germany, and volunteer teachers creating informal learning spaces.

Organizations like World Vision have reached over 2.1 million people in Ukraine, Romania, Moldova, and Georgia with lifesaving aid, shelter, child protection programs, and other essentials as of November 2024. However, my conversations with Ukrainian families reveal persistent gaps in long-term mental health support, particularly for adolescents who struggle with identity formation in displacement.

The impact of conflict on youth displacement is particularly severe because young people often lack the resources and networks that help adults navigate forced movement. They may become separated from families during flight, lack documentation needed for protection, and struggle to access education and services in displacement contexts. Understanding these vulnerabilities is important for developing appropriate support systems.

Persecution and Human Rights Violations:

Political persecution, religious intolerance, ethnic violence, and other human rights violations force many young people from their homes. These forms of displacement often involve targeting based on identity characteristics (ethnicity, religion, political affiliation, and sexual orientation) that are fundamental to who young people understand themselves to be.

Persecution-based displacement often involves particular psychological challenges because it targets young people's core identities and community connections. Talk about religious minorities forced to hide their faith, ethnic groups facing violence, or youth of marginalized races fleeing discrimination—these young people experience displacement as rejection by their home societies, thereby creating complex trauma that affects their sense of belonging and self-worth.

The healing process for persecution-displaced youths often require addressing both trauma and identity affirmation. They need safety and basic services, but they also need communities where their threatened identities can be celebrated rather than hidden. This makes culturally responsive and identity-affirming support particularly crucial for their recovery and development.

Environmental Disasters and Climate Change:

Climate change increasingly drives youth displacement through both sudden-onset disasters like hurricane, flood, and slow-onset changes like drought and sea-level rise. Many youths move in response to inadequate living conditions, unemployment, famines, the effects of climate change, and armed conflicts.

Environmental displacement affects young people in unique ways because it often involves loss of ancestral lands and traditional livelihoods that shape cultural identity. Climate displacement often involves particular uncertainty because environmental changes may be irreversible, making return impossible.

Young people may struggle with grief for lost lands, disrupted cultural practices, and uncertain futures. Their healing often requires processing environmental loss alongside other displacement impacts.

The complexity of climate displacement also lies in its intersection with other factors. Environmental degradation often exacerbates economic hardship, political instability, and social conflict. Young people may experience multiple, layered reasons for displacement that evolve over time, requiring flexible and comprehensive support approaches.

Family Breakdown and Child Protection Issues:

Some young people experience displacement due to family breakdown, abuse, neglect, or other protection concerns. These displaced youth face particular vulnerabilities because they may lack adult advocates and support systems that typically help young people navigate difficult situations.

Unaccompanied and separated children represent a particularly vulnerable subset of displaced youth. Whether separated during flight or displaced independently due to family breakdown, these young people must navigate complex legal, social, and psychological challenges with limited adult support. Their healing often requires not just addressing displacement trauma but building new support networks and developing premature independence skills.

Child protection-related displacement can be particularly complex because the family, which typically provides support during difficult times, may be the source of threat. Young people may experience conflicted feelings about separation from family, guilt about circumstances leading to displacement, and confusion about relationships and trust. Their support needs often extend beyond immediate services to long-term relationship building and identity development.

Historical Perspective On Displacement

**

Indigenous Children and Youth in Canada and the United States:

The systematic removal of Indigenous children from their families and communities represents one of the most devastating examples of state-sanctioned displacement in North American history. Indian children were forcibly abducted by government agents, sent to schools hundreds of miles away, beaten, starved, or otherwise abused when they spoke their Native languages. This wasn't an accidental policy but a deliberate cultural destruction designed to "kill the Indian to save the man."

These residential boarding schools punished Native students for speaking their languages, forced them to take new names, and coerced them to convert to Christianity. Between 1879 and the 1960s, hundreds of thousands of Indigenous children experienced this forced displacement from their families, cultures, and identities.

When I first learned about residential schools through the stories of survivors and their descendants, I was stunned by how this displacement differed from other forms I had studied. This wasn't displacement caused by war or disaster. It was displacement as a weapon, designed to break the transmission of culture, language, and identity from one generation to the next.

In Canada, over 150,000 First Nations, Métis, and Inuit children were forced into residential schools. In the United States, hundreds of boarding schools operated with similar mandates. While children attended federal boarding schools, many endured physical and emotional abuse and, in some cases, died.

The architects of residential school systems were explicit about their intentions. Richard Henry Pratt, founder of the Carlisle Indian Industrial School, famously declared the goal was to "kill the Indian in him, and save the man." This philosophy shaped every aspect of the boarding school experience, from forcible haircuts and uniform clothing to punishment for speaking Native languages and practicing traditional customs.

Children as young as five were removed from their families, often taken without parental consent and sometimes through outright kidnapping by government agents. Families were often forced to send their children to these schools, where they were forbidden to speak their native languages. The distance between schools and home communities was deliberately maintained to prevent family contact and cultural reinforcement.

The daily reality of these institutions involved systematic dehumanization designed to break children's connections to their cultures and identities. Children received new English names, were forbidden to practice traditional ceremonies or customs, and were punished severely for any expression of their Indigenous identities. The curriculum focused on vocational training designed to prepare students for menial labor in the dominant society rather than leadership in their communities.

This system disrupted the intergenerational transmission of parenting knowledge, cultural practices, and community wisdom. Children who spent their formative years in institutions often returned to their communities as strangers, unable to fully reconnect with families and cultural practices they had been forced to abandon.

We may have seen an end to the formal era of residential schools, but Indigenous children and youth continue to experience disproportionate rates of displacement through child welfare systems, juvenile justice systems, and educational institutions that fail to serve them effectively. In Canada, Indigenous children represent about 8% of the child population but account for more than half of children in foster care. In the United States, Native American children are removed from their families at rates significantly higher than non-Native children (Statistics Canada, 2024; National Indian Child Welfare Association, as cited in Montana Courts, n.d.).

This contemporary displacement often perpetuates the same patterns established by historical boarding schools—separation from family and culture, placement in environments that don't understand or value Indigenous identity, and interruption of cultural transmission. While contemporary systems don't explicitly aim for cultural destruction, their impacts can be similarly devastating for Indigenous children and families.

Ukraine:

The Russian invasion of Ukraine in February 2022 created one of the largest displacement crises in recent history, affecting millions of children and youth whose lives were forever altered in a matter of days.

As I write this, Ukrainian children and youth, some of whom I know, continue to navigate the complex realities of war, displacement, and uncertainty about their futures. The number of those displaced hit a record high by the end of 2022 at 117 million, with millions of these being Ukrainian families fleeing the war. Just take a moment to imagine the quick transformation from citizen or resident to refugee.

I have interacted with some youths who had lived or had important business to do in Ukraine before the war, and they often describe this sudden transformation as surreal, like waking up in someone else's life. Unlike displacement that builds gradually due to economic hardship or environmental changes, war displacement often happens with shocking suddenness, leaving children and youth with little time to process what's happening or prepare psychologically for the journey ahead.

The educational disruption alone affects millions of Ukrainian children, youths, and foreign students. Schools became targets, underground shelters became classrooms, and education systems had to be rebuilt virtually overnight. I remember a young and promising African youth who had gained admission into a university in Kyiv. He had barely completed his first year when everything changed, and he had to make the difficult decision of terminating his scholarship at the institution.

Students approaching graduation face uncertainty about whether their Ukrainian credentials will be recognized, whether they should pursue education in host countries, and whether they'll be able to return to Ukraine to complete their studies. This uncertainty affects motivation and mental health, as young people struggle to plan for futures that feel completely unpredictable.

While online Ukrainian schools have continued operating, not all displaced families have reliable internet access or appropriate devices for multiple children. I've worked with families where teenagers share one phone to attend online classes, creating additional stress and limiting educational access.

The trauma of sudden separation as a result of the displacement crisis became the order of the day in many Ukrainian families. The uncertainty surrounding family reunion created additional stress. Unlike other forms of displacement where families typically move together, Ukrainian children often don't know when or if they'll be reunited with their fathers and older male relatives. This uncertainty affects their ability to process their displacement and plan for their futures.

The psychological impact of war and displacement on Ukrainian children manifests in various ways, from acute stress reactions to longer-term adaptation challenges. Many children and youths, as expected, exhibit symptoms of hypervigilance, struggling to relax in new environments and constantly looking out for danger signs. Air raid sirens, loud noises, and crowded spaces can trigger intense anxiety responses. Sleep disturbances are nearly universal among Ukrainian youth. Nightmares about war, worry about family members, and adjustment to new environments combine to disrupt rest.

However, we cannot but observe the remarkable resilience and coping strategies among Ukrainian youth. Many channel their experiences into advocacy and activism, using their voices to raise awareness about the war's impact on children. Others focus intensively on maintaining Ukrainian cultural practices and language as ways of preserving their identity. Some develop protective strategies for younger siblings and friends, finding strength through caring for others.

European countries have demonstrated remarkable solidarity in welcoming Ukrainian refugees, but the scale of the crisis has also revealed gaps and challenges in integration support. Different countries have adopted varying approaches, from immediate school enrollment to specialized programs for Ukrainian students.

Poland, which has received the largest number of Ukrainian refugees, has created both Ukrainian-language schools and integration programs in Polish schools. I've observed how these different approaches affect children differently—some thrive in Ukrainian-language environments that preserve cultural continuity, while others prefer Polish schools that facilitate faster integration.

Germany has developed comprehensive support systems, including trauma counseling, language support, and family services. However, bureaucratic processes can be overwhelming for displaced families already dealing with trauma and uncertainty.

The generosity of host communities in all of these has been extraordinary, with many families opening their homes and volunteers providing translation, tutoring, and emotional support. However, cultural differences and communication challenges sometimes create tension. Understanding these dynamics is therefore necessary for supporting both Ukrainian families and host communities in building positive relationships.

Democratic Republic of Congo

In the eastern regions of the Democratic Republic of Congo, there have been reports of displacement characterized by protracted conflict, and limited international attention. The children and youth affected by ongoing violence in DRC face challenges that differ significantly from those experiencing sudden displacement due to acute crises like the war in Ukraine.

Unlike the highly visible Ukrainian crisis, displacement in eastern DRC often occurs in contexts of ongoing, cyclical violence that has persisted for decades. Children grow up experiencing multiple displacements, returning to destroyed communities, and facing constant uncertainty about safety and stability. This protracted nature of conflict creates unique psychological and developmental challenges.

The ongoing nature of conflict in DRC means that displacement often lacks clear beginning and end points. Families may return to communities multiple times, only to flee again when violence resurges. Children develop complex relationships with place and home, learning to maintain psychological flexibility while grieving repeated losses.

Educational disruption in protracted displacement contexts is particularly severe. Unlike Ukrainian children who may continue education online or in host country schools, many Congolese children experience years-long interruptions in schooling. Schools are often targets of violence, teachers flee alongside communities, and educational infrastructure is repeatedly destroyed and rebuilt.

One of the most devastating aspects of displacement in eastern DRC was the recruitment of children into armed groups and the widespread use of sexual violence as a weapon of war. These experiences created trauma that extended far beyond typical displacement impacts.

Children recruited into armed groups faced forced participation in violence that violated their moral development and created profound psychological wounds. Boys as young as eight were given weapons and forced to commit acts that contradicted their natural inclinations toward play and learning. Girls faced sexual violence and forced marriages within armed groups, disrupting their physical, emotional, and social development.

In situations like this, the stigma associated with recruitment and sexual violence compounds the trauma. Communities may reject children who return from armed groups, viewing them as contaminated or dangerous. Girls who have experienced sexual violence may face rejection from families and communities, creating additional displacement from social support systems.

Pathways To Healing

Moving forward, we must fundamentally shift our approach to include children and youths as genuine partners in designing interventions, not just passive recipients of adult decisions. This means creating spaces where young voices are not only heard but actively sought out and valued. Young people need to be at the planning table, and not just sit on the chairs we have arranged for them. Too often, healing programs are designed without meaningful input from the children and communities they aim to serve. I've witnessed countless well-intentioned interventions fail because they were built on assumptions rather than authentic understanding of what children and families actually needed.

We also need to (truly) listen to what young people need, rather than what we adults think they need. I have learned that children often have profound insights into their own healing needs. When given opportunities to express themselves through art, storytelling, play, or direct conversation, they frequently identify solutions that adults overlook entirely. Their perspectives can reveal healing pathways that no textbook could have taught us.

Governments must invest in conflict prevention through genuine diplomacy and justice initiatives that address underlying tensions before they explode into violence. It means supporting climate adaptation strategies that help communities stay in their ancestral lands rather than being forced to flee environmental disasters. It means promoting economic development that provides real alternatives to forced migration, creating opportunities that allow families to thrive where they are.

Social justice initiatives that address the inequality and oppression that often drive displacement should be prioritized. When children are forced to flee because of persecution, poverty, or violence, healing their individual trauma while ignoring these systemic causes is like putting a bandage on a wound that keeps reopening. This doesn't mean abandoning immediate healing interventions for displaced children who need support right now. Rather, it means embedding these interventions within broader social change efforts, understanding that individual healing and systemic change must happen simultaneously to create lasting transformation.

One of the damaging myths in humanitarian work is that displacement trauma can be healed quickly with short-term interventions. I've seen too many programs that swoop in during a crisis, provide intensive support for a few months, and then disappear just as children are beginning to trust and open up. Healing from displacement trauma is not a sprint; it's more like learning to tend a garden that will grow for years. Effective approaches require sustained commitment that extends far beyond the initial crisis response. Children need to know that the adults supporting them won't vanish the moment funding cycles change or media attention shifts elsewhere.

Essentially, this means developing relationship-based interventions that provide ongoing support as children grow and their needs evolve. A child who needs play therapy at age seven might need career counseling at seventeen, but the relationship that makes both interventions possible is the constant thread connecting these different phases of healing. It also means investing in community capacity building that creates local healing infrastructure. Rather than creating dependency on outside experts, we should be training community members to provide ongoing support, ensuring that healing resources remain available long after external programs end.

While we must acknowledge trauma and its very real impacts, our healing approaches cannot be built entirely on deficit models that see displaced children primarily as damaged or broken. This perspective, however well-intentioned, can actually reinforce the very powerlessness that trauma creates. Instead, we need to recognize the existing strengths that children, families, and communities possess. Every child or youth who has survived displacement has also developed remarkable capabilities in the process. They've learned to adapt to new environments, often mastering new languages and navigating unfamiliar systems with skills that would challenge most adults.

This means celebrating the resilience and survival skills that children have developed, helping them see their adaptation abilities as evidence of their strength rather than just symptoms of their trauma. A child who has learned to be hypervigilant in dangerous situations has developed a valuable skill; our job is to help them learn when and how to use it, not to simply eliminate it.

We also need to support the natural healing processes that are already happening rather than pathologizing normal responses to abnormal situations. When children show signs of grief, anger, or hypervigilance after experiencing displacement, these are often healthy responses to unhealthy circumstances, not mental illnesses that need to be cured.

Displaced children and youths exist in complex relationships with time that can feel overwhelming and disorienting. They carry memories of what they've lost, struggle with the challenges of their current situation, and face uncertainty about what lies ahead. This temporal displacement can be just as traumatic as physical displacement.

Effective healing approaches must help children honor what was lost without getting stuck in endless grief. This means creating spaces where children can remember and mourn their former homes, communities, and ways of life while also investing energy in their current reality. It's not about forgetting the past but about integrating it into a larger story that includes possibility for the future.

We need to build capacity for current challenges while maintaining hope for what's possible ahead. Children need practical skills for navigating their new environments, but they also need to believe that their current struggles are not permanent, that they have agency in shaping what comes next.

This is very important. We must support identity development that encompasses multiple cultural influences without forcing children to fragment themselves. A child or youth can be proudly Somali and confidently American, deeply connected to Islamic traditions and fluent in secular academic environments. Identity doesn't have to be singular or simple; it can be beautifully complex and multifaceted.

The goal isn't to help these children and youths return to who they were before displacement or to completely reinvent themselves in their new context. Instead, it is to support them in becoming who they're meant to be, integrating all their experiences into a coherent sense of self that honors their journey while embracing their potential.

Reflections And Conclusion

After years of working with displaced children across different contexts, I find myself constantly humbled by their resilience and wisdom. Each child and youth I've worked with has taught me something new about healing, survival, and hope.

Irrespective of cultural contexts, children and youth around the world share fundamental needs of safety, connection, understanding, and hope for the future. They play, laugh, dream, and love in remarkably similar ways, even under the most difficult circumstances. This universality reminds me that while our approaches must be culturally specific, our commitment to supporting children's well-being transcends all boundaries.

Individual therapy, while valuable, pales in comparison to the healing power of supportive communities. The children who heal most successfully are those surrounded by adults who care about them, peers who understand their experiences, and communities that welcome their contributions. This understanding has shifted my practice from individual-focused interventions to community-building approaches that create healing environments for all children, not just those identified as "traumatized."

Children heal better when they maintain connections to their cultural heritage while adapting to new environments. This isn't about preserving culture in museum-like ways, but about supporting living, evolving cultural practices that provide identity and meaning. I have learned to ask not just "How can we help this child heal?" but "How can we help this child remain connected to who they are while becoming who they need to be?"

Working with displaced children has taught me to sit with unresolved grief—both theirs and my own. Not everything can be fixed, not every loss can be recovered, and not every trauma can be fully healed. Learning to hold space for ongoing pain while nurturing hope for the future is perhaps the most important skill I have developed. This acceptance doesn't lead to resignation, but rather to a deeper compassion and more sustainable approach to healing work.

So, as we move forward in this work as social workers, we must remember that healing is not about returning to some original state. That is impossible after displacement. Instead, it's about creating new possibilities that integrate loss and gain, memory, hope, individual strength and community support.

The children we serve today will become tomorrow's healers, leaders, and bridge-builders. Our responsibility is not to fix them or save them, but to walk alongside them as they discover their own paths to healing and wholeness. In doing so, we too are healed, and the larger human community is strengthened.

In the end, healing for children and youth who have found themselves across borders is all about supporting and creating a world where every child and youth can thrive, where diversity is celebrated, where forced displacement becomes unnecessary, and where our shared humanity creates bridges stronger than the forces that divide us.

CHAPTER TEN
HEALING FOR FAMILIES IN CRIME OR MILITARY ZONES

> *"When supporting children from military families or families living in high-crime or war-affected zones, we must recognize that these children often experience the psychological toll of their environment. Though they may not directly face the same events, the emotional and psychological impact—known in social work as vicarious trauma—manifests through their close connection to those enduring trauma."* - Eseosa Omoregie

Serving one's country is far from an easy task. It demands a unique kind of selflessness, especially when it involves making the ultimate sacrifice. To willingly place oneself in harm's way for the protection of national ideals and freedoms is an extraordinary commitment, and I greatly salute every great patriot committed to this.

Now, imagine giving your all—mentally, emotionally, and physically—only to return home and find nothing familiar to fall back on. Your spouse seems distant. Your children don't know how to engage with you. For dual-serving families, the reality can be even harsher.

What does it mean for a child to grow up not knowing if their parent (or both parents) will return home safe or emotionally whole?

Have you ever wondered what this does to their development and sense of security? Even when service members do return, many carry invisible wounds, such as PTSD, that often go unspoken yet deeply impact family dynamics. These unhealed traumas can ripple into the next generation, unintentionally shaping how children see the world, relationships, and themselves.

Some children experience what is called vicarious trauma, that is, the emotional residue of exposure to trauma experienced by someone close to them. This is not always obvious and might show up as withdrawal, anxiety, or sudden anger.

How do we support these children, who are often expected to carry on as if nothing has changed? How do different countries respond?

What lessons can be drawn from policies in Canada, the United States, Nigeria, and the Middle East? What psychological and social services are available? How does culture shape how we support, or fail to support these families?

In this chapter, we will explore what systems of support exist for military families, especially focusing on the children and youth. I will begin with this story gathered from an interview with a survivor of the Boko Haram crisis in Nigeria.

Let's call this lady Amina (not her real name).

Living With Crime And Terror In Mind
(A case study from Nigeria)

(Amina's Story)

Being a social worker can sometimes put you in the position of a journalist, just as it did on this day when I met with Amina. Having been born and brought up in Northern Nigeria, Amina experienced firsthand the genesis and growth of insurgent attacks in the region.

According to her, it all began on the 18th of February, 2006. What looked like a peaceful demonstration in the state was hijacked, and later escalated to a full-blown riot where people were killed, houses and properties were burnt, and the entire state was thrown into pandemonium.

Her mother had gone to the market that very morning, but had to return so soon with a report that the town was not safe. This went on for an undefined period, but through the intervention of mobile policemen, the situation was controlled for a while.

However, in 2010, there was a resurgence of this attack, but this time, the insurgents came strictly for the mobile policemen. They targeted their operational base, armed with sophisticated guns and improvised explosive devices that could not match what the uniform men had at their disposal. As a result, there was such a bloodbath, and so many mobile policemen were killed.

What happened was that the insurgents resurfaced without a hint, and met the uniform men unprepared. Turns out, they had not made use of available weapons for quite a long time, so their response to the insurgents was weak. According to Amina's description, the crime scene was a terrible sight. The situation escalated, and the military had to come in.

But how did this all happen?

Before the resurgence of this attack in 2010, a man named Muhammed Yusuf went around town announcing that Western education is forbidden. This was the philosophy that birthed the name Boko Haram. What he did was to go street by street, speaking to young people to abandon Western education.

As he progressed in this mission, many youths began to listen to him and truly abandoned their pursuit of Western education. Those who had earned certificates tore and burned theirs, and ended becoming followers of this man, Muhammed Yusuf. This was in 2009.

This continued for months, and it was later discovered that he (Muhammed Yusuf) had an underground building where he gathered these youths and recruited them into learning how to shoot, and operate other dangerous weapons. He got youths from everywhere around town to join in doing these.

Muhammed's mission, as Amina briefed, was to put an end to Western education. One of the philosophies they believed was that even if they die in battle, they will go to heaven and will have seven virgins to themselves as a reward. This indoctrination gave the recruits enough reason to give themselves up for suicide bombing missions.

Speaking of her experience as a survivor, she couldn't use words to convey the trauma and fear she and her family faced during the heat of the insurgent attacks. She talked about developing a "tough skin" after it seemed to become a norm in the region.

According to her, they lived with the consciousness that any one of them could die at any moment, be it at home (because they actually dropped bombs in houses) or while they stepped out. So, the practice was to say their last prayers before leaving their homes, and each time they returned in one piece, that was considered a miracle. This normalization of terror became a coping mechanism. Their minds, she explained, had to adapt to survive the unpredictable bombing routine.

Exploring Support Structures For Affected Families
(Case Studies from Different Nations)

Nigeria

Amina's experience, though extreme, highlights something important about how children and youth adapt to violence and uncertainty, whether from insurgency, war, or military deployment. In Nigeria, as in many cultures, military families are conditioned differently from civilian ones. Fathers in active service live with the consciousness that death is an occupational hazard, and when it comes, it's often viewed as honorable service to the nation.

Their children grow up understanding that parents can be called to duty at any moment and might never return. This isn't a substitute for grief and trauma, but it does serve as what one military counselor described to me as "psychological preparation for harsh realities."

This cultural conditioning raises important questions about how different societies prepare their children for military-related loss and trauma. The approaches vary dramatically across nations, as I discovered while researching support systems in Canada, the United States, and Afghanistan.

In Nigeria, there are policies put in place by the government to support families of military veterans. The first is educational sponsorship. Currently, this intervention spans till the child or children of military parents reach the age of 21. There are stringent procedures that must be followed to get this, because many families claim to send their children to school but end up misappropriating the academic funds. So, there has to be proof that shows that the children are truly schooling.

Then, there is death benefit. This is compensation for the death of any father who dies while in active service. Many families depend on their husbands to provide food and other family necessities, and their death is like cutting off their only source of income.

There is also NHIS (National Health Insurance Scheme) that provides access to free medical care. Sometimes this may not totally be free, especially in situations when the facility doesn't have what is needed for their treatment. They will need to purchase from another source, then request payment.

For the widows of military veterans, there's a widow's association through which incentives from the government can come in at any time. However, to be a beneficiary of this, widows must belong to the Legion circle.

There are also policies that allow for the employment of children of military veterans, but the implementation rate of this very policy, as gathered from families, seems to be very low.

Canada

Canada has developed what many experts consider a gold standard for military family support. The Canadian Armed Forces (CAF) provides multiple layers of assistance specifically designed for children and families facing deployment stress and trauma.

Take the case of the Morrison family from Petawawa, Ontario. When Captain Sarah Morrison was deployed to Latvia in 2023, her husband, Mark, became the primary caregiver for their two children, ages seven and twelve. What struck me about their story was how seamlessly they were connected to support services.

Through the Canadian Forces Morale and Welfare Services (CFMWS), Mark accessed immediate childcare support, mental health counseling for both children, and family peer support coordination (Canadian Armed Forces, 2024). The Operational Stress Injury Social Support (OSISS) program provided a family peer support coordinator who helped connect them to community resources and ongoing mental health services.

Research from Queen's University found that Canadian adolescents in military families show increased risk for poor mental health, but peer support appears to play a protective role (Coulthard et al., 2023). The Canadian system recognizes this, integrating peer support directly into their service delivery model.

Dr. Lisa Sinclair, a researcher studying Canadian military families, notes that their approach addresses what she calls "the whole family ecosystem" rather than treating service members in isolation (Canadian Paediatric Society, 2017). This includes specialized training for pediatric care providers to recognize the unique challenges military children face, from frequent relocations to parental deployment anxiety.

United States

The U.S. approach has evolved significantly since the Iraq and Afghanistan conflicts, driven partly by the sobering realization that military children were experiencing unprecedented levels of stress and trauma.

Dr. Maria Rodriguez, a family therapist at Fort Bragg, shared the story of the Johnson family. Staff Sergeant Mike Johnson returned from his third deployment to Afghanistan in 2019 with severe PTSD. His two teenagers, Ashley and David, had developed what clinicians call "anticipatory grief"—mourning their father while he was still alive but emotionally unavailable.

"The kids knew something was different about Dad," Dr. Rodriguez explained. "Ashley started having panic attacks before school, and David became aggressive with classmates. They were living with a version of their father who looked the same but felt like a stranger."

The family was connected to the National Child Traumatic Stress Network's evidence-based interventions, specifically designed for military families. The program focuses on trauma-informed care that recognizes how parental PTSD affects entire family systems.

Additionally, programs like the Iraq and Afghanistan Service Grant provide educational support, with maximum awards of $7,395 for children of fallen service members for the 2024-2025 academic year. These financial supports recognize that healing extends beyond mental health into educational and developmental opportunities.

Afghanistan

Perhaps nowhere is the need for child-focused trauma support more urgent than in Afghanistan itself. Since the Taliban's return to power in 2021, the situation for children has become increasingly dire.

I connected virtually with Dr. Ahmad Shahir, a pediatric psychiatrist who worked with international NGOs in Kabul before the current crisis. He described treating children who, like Amina in Nigeria, had normalized violence and lived in constant fear. "We had children as young as six who would flinch at the sound of aircraft overhead," Dr. Shahir recalled.

The international response has focused on humanitarian aid, but Dr. Shahir emphasized that mental health support for children remains critically underfunded. "Physical survival comes first, but we cannot ignore the psychological wounds that will shape an entire generation." Organizations like UNICEF continue to work with partners to support children and their families across the country, though access remains severely limited (UNICEF, 2024).

Healing: The Heart of the Matter

When a parent is whole, their children have a better chance at being whole too. And when children are supported, they are more resilient, more compassionate, and better equipped to thrive in society.

When supporting children from military families or families living in high-crime or war-affected zones, we must recognize that these children often experience the psychological toll of their environment. Though they may not directly face the same events, the emotional and psychological impact known in social work as vicarious trauma, manifests through their close connection to those enduring trauma. This form of secondary exposure can be as damaging as direct experience, as supported by research on intergenerational trauma and stress contagion within families.

So, how do we ensure that no child pays the emotional and all-round cost of national service alone? How do we build systems that don't just honor service in ceremony but support it in practice?

These are the questions we will dive into in this section, so whether you are a policymaker, educator, health provider, or simply a concerned citizen, this topic invites all of us to reflect, to empathize, and most importantly, to act.

Mental Health Services:

Through my research across these three contexts, several key principles emerged for effective mental health support for military and conflict-affected children, with Trauma-Informed Care as the foundation. Three countries (Canada, the United States, and international organizations working in Afghanistan) have developed effective programs that emphasize trauma-informed approaches to healing. These approaches recognize how exposure to violence or parental trauma affects child development.

Effective and age-appropriate programs that tailor their approaches to the developmental stages of this demographic are also necessary. Young children might engage in play therapy that helps them process experiences they can't yet verbalize. Adolescents often benefit from group interventions where they can connect with peers facing similar challenges.

Also, interventions must be such that treats or helps the entire family heal, rather than individual members in isolation. When a parent heals from Post-Traumatic Stress Disorder (PTSD), children often show improvement even without direct intervention.

Respite and Emergency Care:

When both parents serve or when a single parent lacks support, the question of who steps in becomes critical. The answers vary dramatically across systems.

In Canada, the CFMWS provides comprehensive emergency childcare services and has formal agreements with community organizations to ensure continuity of care during deployments. Military families have access to subsidized childcare and emergency respite services that understand the unpredictable nature of military life.

The U.S. system is more fragmented, with significant variation between bases and regions. Some installations have robust family readiness groups and formal respite programs, while others rely heavily on informal support networks that can be inconsistent.

In conflict zones like northern Nigeria or Afghanistan, formal respite care is often nonexistent. Families rely on extended family networks and community support systems that may themselves be under threat. Amina's family, for instance, had to rely on relatives in other regions and sometimes took refuge in the church or military camp.

Community and Cultural Healing Approaches:

One of the most powerful insights from my research was how different cultures integrate traditional healing practices with clinical care.

In Nigeria, Amina described how community storytelling sessions helped children process their experiences. "When the situation in town was a bit relaxed, there were times my grandparents would gather us and tell stories about the civil war and how they managed to live through those times." According to her, those stories did not directly address what they were going through, but they understood the messages about resilience and survival.

Canadian Indigenous military families often incorporate traditional healing circles and elder guidance into their recovery processes. The Canadian Armed Forces has begun formally recognizing and supporting these culturally specific approaches.

In Afghanistan, Dr. Shahir noted that poetry and music had traditionally played important roles in processing trauma, though these practices became restricted under Taliban rule. "Families would create private spaces for traditional expressions of grief and healing, but always with the fear of being discovered."

The integration of cultural healing practices with clinical interventions appears to strengthen outcomes across all contexts. Children who can access both traditional and modern healing modalities often show greater resilience and faster recovery.

Educational Support Systems:

Schools play a crucial role in supporting military children, but the level of training and awareness varies dramatically.

In Canada, the Department of National Defence works directly with school systems in military communities to provide specialized support services. Teachers receive training to recognize signs of deployment stress and trauma in students.

The U.S. Military Child Education Coalition has developed comprehensive resources for educators, but implementation depends heavily on local buy-in and resources. Schools near major military installations often have robust support programs, while those in areas with smaller military populations may lack specialized knowledge.

In conflict-affected areas, schools themselves often become targets or are forced to close entirely. Amina recalled how her education was repeatedly interrupted: "We would start a semester, then have to flee when attacks intensified. Some of my coursemates never returned to school after their families relocated." However, in Nigeria, there is funding made available for the children of soldiers who haven't crossed the age of 21.

Educational continuity emerges as both a practical necessity and a psychological anchor for children experiencing instability. When everything else is uncertain, school can provide structure and normalcy, if it is available and safe.

Supporting Military Families: Practical Strategies for Healing

Drawing from the framework developed by the National Child Traumatic Stress Network and my observations across different contexts, several key strategies emerge for supporting military families and their children:

The well-being of the at-home parent or caregiver fundamentally shapes how children cope during transitions like deployment (National Child Traumatic Stress Network, 2024). This insight proved consistent across all the families I interviewed.

As the NCTSN emphasizes, caregivers need time to process major transitions themselves before helping children navigate them. This might mean having private conversations with trusted adults before sharing news with children. Mark Morrison, the Canadian military spouse I interviewed, described taking a full day to process his wife's deployment news before sitting down with their children.

201

Successful families proactively identify and secure additional resources needed to maintain family routines. This includes childcare arrangements, financial planning, and establishing support networks. The key is planning these supports before they're needed, not during crisis moments.

Maintaining physical health, mental health, work-life balance, and community connections becomes even more critical during family separations. Strategies like stress management techniques, regular physical activity, gratitude practices, and acts of kindness toward others all contribute to family resilience.

Also, staying attuned to your own mental health helps caregivers recognize when they need different coping strategies or additional support. This self-awareness models emotional intelligence for children, and prevents caregiver burnout.

When it has to do with creating deployment plans, early preparation and planning are essential for maintaining children's well-being throughout deployment processes (National Child Traumatic Stress Network, 2024). Families need concrete plans for how and how often they'll maintain contact with deployed parents. Technology has revolutionized these possibilities, but successful families establish routines and backup plans for when technology fails.

Discussing what families know about upcoming deployments, acknowledging the difficulty for everyone involved, and explaining available support systems helps children feel prepared rather than blindsided. For families with multiple deployment experiences, it's important to acknowledge how current news might trigger memories of previous experiences.

Parents and partners must ensure that major changes like school transfers or temporary living arrangements are discussed. Question-and-answer sessions should be held, and there should be an honest acknowledgment of the challenging nature of each move. Children cope better when they understand the reasoning behind changes and have opportunities to express their concerns.

Creating new calendars and daily routines helps children understand what their lives will look like during deployment periods. This includes discussing new activities, caregiving arrangements, and dedicated family time.

Lastly, children worry about deployed parents' safety, and they need honest reassurance about training and preparation without unrealistic guarantees. Reminding children of their support networks and the people who care about them provides security without false certainty about outcomes.

Beyond the NCTSN framework, my research revealed several other crucial support strategies:

Peer Support Networks: Both Canadian and U.S. programs emphasize connecting military children with peers facing similar experiences. These connections reduce isolation and normalize their experiences.

Cultural Integration: Successful programs incorporate families' cultural backgrounds and healing traditions alongside clinical interventions. This might include storytelling, spiritual practices, or community gatherings.

Educational Advocacy: Schools need training to recognize and respond to the unique challenges military children face. This includes understanding the impact of frequent moves, deployment stress, and potential trauma exposure.

Economic Security: Financial stress compounds the emotional challenges military families face. Programs addressing educational costs, emergency financial assistance, and long-term economic planning significantly impact family well-being.

Lessons from Global Experiences

Comparing approaches across Nigeria, Canada, the United States, and Afghanistan reveals both universal principles and cultural specificities in supporting military children and conflict survivors. Certain elements appear crucial regardless of context—early intervention, family-centered approaches, trauma-informed care, and integration of cultural healing practices with clinical support.

Effective programs respect and incorporate local healing traditions, communication styles, and family structures rather than imposing external models. Also, I have to reiterate that there is no one size fits all when it has to do with healing. The most successful approaches coordinate across military, healthcare, educational, and community systems rather than working in isolation.

Healing from military-related trauma and deployment stress should be viewed from a long-term perspective. That is to say, healing is an ongoing process that requires sustained support, not just crisis intervention.

Amina's reflection on her healing journey illustrates this long-term perspective: "Relocation to a new and peaceful environment helped, but there was always that suspicion that too much peace might mean danger was coming. Time has been the greatest healer, but I still have occasional fears of loud noises. Getting engaged with meaningful work and creative activities have also helped me heal from the past."

Her experience, and the stories from other world contexts, portray an important lesson: that getting back on form happens gradually, through setbacks and breakthroughs, and requires multiple types of support over time.

Reflections and Conclusions

If you're reading this as a military parent, caregiver, or family member, I want you to know that your experiences matter, and your struggles are real. Whether you're dealing with deployment stress, combat trauma, or the ongoing challenges of military life, you're not alone in this journey.

To the service members reading this: Your sacrifice extends beyond your individual service. When you serve, your entire family serves alongside you. The visible and invisible wounds you carry are not signs of weakness but normal responses to abnormal situations. Seeking help isn't failing your mission, but it's a way of completing it by ensuring your family can heal together.

To the spouses and partners, I admire your strength in holding families together during times of deployments, relocations, and reintegration. It is extraordinary. But please, remember that caring for everyone else doesn't mean neglecting yourself. The research consistently shows that your well-being directly impacts your children's ability to cope, so taking time for your own healing isn't selfish but essential.

To the children and young adults in military families: Your experiences of worry, anger, confusion, or sadness about your family's military life are completely understandable. It's okay to feel proud of your parents' service while simultaneously wishing things were different. It's normal to feel anxious during deployments or to struggle with frequent moves. These feelings don't make you ungrateful or weak; they make you human.

You didn't choose military life, but it has shaped you in ways both challenging and strengthening. Many of you develop resilience, adaptability, and maturity beyond your years. These are gifts, but they shouldn't come at the cost of your childhood or mental health.

To all military families: Healing is possible, but it often requires reaching out for support. Whether that's through formal programs like those available in Canada and the United States, community support networks, cultural healing practices, or professional mental health services, help is available. You don't have to navigate this journey alone. Your service matters. Your sacrifices have meaning. Your family's journey toward healing honors that service while building something hopeful for the future. The goal isn't to erase difficult experiences, but to ensure they don't define your family's story, going forward.

To the broader community reading this: Military families are in your neighborhoods, schools, and communities. They often bear their burdens quietly, not wanting to be seen as seeking special attention. But they need our support—not just our gratitude, but our genuine care and practical assistance. This means supporting initiatives that fund military family services, volunteering with organizations that serve military children, or simply being aware of the unique challenges these families face. When you encounter a military child who seems withdrawn or anxious, remember that their behavior might reflect experiences far beyond typical childhood stresses.

The healing of military families isn't just a military issue but a societal responsibility. When we support these families effectively, we honor service while building stronger communities for everyone.

As I finish writing this chapter, I'm amazed by how often the families I interviewed spoke about hope despite trauma, connection despite separation, and healing despite wounds that may never fully close. Their stories remind us that while we cannot always prevent trauma, we can always choose how we respond to it.

The path forward requires all of us, and that includes military families seeking healing, communities providing support, policymakers ensuring resources, and individuals offering understanding. Together, we can ensure that no child pays the emotional cost of national service alone, and no family has to navigate the journey toward healing without support.

Ultimately, healing is possible when we commit to supporting one another through the darkness and towards the light.

REFERENCES

4 Common Parenting Styles: Authoritative, Authoritarian, Permissive, Uninvolved. (2025, March 18). Today. https://www.today.com/parents/parenting-styles-authoritative-authoritarian-permissive-uninvolved-rcna194121

Aboriginal Justice. (n.d.). Underlying causes of Aboriginal over-representation. Aboriginal Justice. https://www.aboriginaljustice.vic.gov.au/the-agreement/aboriginal-over-representation-in-the-justice-system/underlying-causes-of-aboriginal

Albrecht, G. L., & Devlieger, P. J. (1999). The disability paradox: High quality of life against all odds. Social Science & Medicine, 48(8), 977-988.

American Psychological Association. (2020). Publication manual of the American Psychological Association (7th ed.). American Psychological Association.

American Psychological Association. (2023). Trauma-informed approaches to adolescent relationship abuse and sexual violence prevention. Journal of Adolescent Health.

American Psychological Association Foundation. (n.d.). Trauma-informed juvenile justice. https://www.apaf.org/our-programs/justice/free-resources/trauma-informed-juvenile-justice/

Association of Orphanages and Home Operators in Nigeria (ASOHON). (2023). Strengthening Nigeria's foster care system. ASOHON Publications.

Australian Institute of Family Studies. (2018). Principles of trauma-informed approaches to child sexual abuse. Government Publication.

Australian Institute of Health and Welfare. (n.d.). 2.11 Contact with the criminal justice system. Indigenous Health and Welfare Performance Framework. https://www.indigenoushpf.gov.au/measures/2-11-contact-with-the-criminal-justice-system

Authoritarian parenting style. (n.d.). MSU Extension. https://www.canr.msu.edu/news/authoritarian_parenting_style

Babson, K. A., & Feldner, M. T. (2010). Temporal relations between sleep problems and both traumatic event exposure and PTSD: A critical review of the empirical literature. Journal of Anxiety Disorders, 24(1), 1-15.

Baumrind's Parenting Styles – Parenting and Family Diversity Issues. (2020, May 18). Iowa State University Digital Press. https://iastate.pressbooks.pub/parentingfamilydiversity/chapter/chapter-1-2/

Brave Heart, M. Y. H. (2003). The historical trauma response among natives and its relationship with substance abuse: A Lakota illustration. Journal of Psychoactive Drugs, 35(1), 7-13.

British Council. (n.d.). How traditional justice in Nigeria is changing. Voices Magazine. https://www.britishcouncil.org/voices-magazine/how-traditional-justice-nigeria-changing

Campbell, R., Dworkin, E., & Cabral, G. (2009). An ecological model of the impact of sexual assault on women's mental health. Trauma, Violence, & Abuse, 10(3), 225-246.

Canadian Armed Forces. (2024). Additional mental health resources for CAF members and their families. Government of Canada. https://www.canada.ca/en/department-national-defence/services/benefits-military/health-support/mental-health/programs-and-services.html

Canadian Encyclopedia. (n.d.). Intergenerational trauma and residential schools.

https://www.thecanadianencyclopedia.ca/en/article/intergenerational-trauma-and-residential-schools

Canadian Paediatric Society. (2017). Caring for children and youth from Canadian military families: Special considerations. Paediatrics & Child Health, 22(2), e1-e8. https://doi.org/10.1093/pch/pxx033

Center for Justice Innovation. (n.d.). Restorative justice. https://www.innovatingjustice.org/areas-of-focus/restorative-justice

Centers for Disease Control and Prevention. (2022). Preventing sexual violence. https://www.cdc.gov/violenceprevention/sexualviolence/fastfact.html

Chapin Hall at the University of Chicago. (2017). Missed opportunities: LGBTQ youth homelessness in America. True Colors United.

Chassin, L. (2008). Juvenile justice and substance use. Future of Children, 18(2), 165-183.

Child Welfare Information Gateway. (2019). What is child abuse and neglect? Recognizing the signs and symptoms. U.S. Department of Health and Human Services, Children's Bureau.

Children's Aid Society of Toronto. (2024). Supporting Black children and families in care. Retrieved from https://www.torontocas.ca

Church World Service. (n.d.). Healing hearts: Ukrainian children find hope amidst war trauma. CWS Global. https://cwsglobal.org/blog/healing-hearts-ukrainian-children-find-hope-amidst-war-trauma/

Clawson, H. J., Dutch, N., Solomon, A., & Grace, L. G. (2009). Human trafficking into and within the United States: A review of the literature. U.S. Department of Health and Human Services.

Cook, A., Spinazzola, J., Ford, J., Lanktree, C., Blaustein, M., Cloitre, M., ... & Mallah, K. (2017). Complex trauma in children and adolescents. Psychiatric Annals, 35(5), 390-398.

Coulthard, H., Harms, C. A., Morley, C., et al. (2023). Adolescent mental health in military families: Evidence from the Canadian Health Behaviour in School-aged Children study. Canadian Journal of Public Health, 114(3), 412-422.

Curtis, R., Terry, K., Dank, M., Dombrowski, K., & Khan, B. (2008). The commercial sexual exploitation of children in New York City, Volume One: The CSEC population in New York City: Size, characteristics, and needs. Center for Court Innovation.

Danieli, Y. (Ed.). (1998). International handbook of multigenerational legacies of trauma. Springer.

Darkness to Light. (2015). Child sexual abuse statistics. https://www.d2l.org/wp-content/uploads/2017/01/all_statistics_20150619.pdf

Department of Justice Canada. (2025, March 10). Canada's first federal Indigenous Justice Strategy to address systemic discrimination and overrepresentation in the Canadian justice system. https://www.canada.ca/en/department-justice/news/2025/03/canadas-first-federal-indigenous-justice-strategy-to-address-systemic-discrimination-and-overrepresentation-in-the-canadian-justice-system.html

Department of Justice Canada. (n.d.). Causes of overrepresentation. Overrepresentation of Indigenous People in the Canadian Criminal Justice System: Causes and Responses. https://www.justice.gc.ca/eng/rp-pr/jr/oip-cjs/p4.html

Department of Justice Canada. (n.d.). Engagement findings – Black youth and the criminal justice system: Summary report of an engagement process in Canada. https://www.justice.gc.ca/eng/rp-pr/jr/bycjs-yncjs/engagement-resultat.html

Department of Justice Canada. (n.d.). Restorative justice. https://www.justice.gc.ca/eng/cj-jp/rj-jr/index.html

Department of Justice Canada. (n.d.). Understanding the overrepresentation of Indigenous people. State of the Criminal Justice System Dashboard. https://www.justice.gc.ca/socjs-esjp/en/ind-aut/uo-cs

Drug Abuse Statistics. (2024, May 2). Teenage drug use statistics [2023]: Data & trends on abuse. https://drugabusestatistics.org/teen-drug-use/

Dube, S. R., Anda, R. F., Whitfield, C. L., Brown, D. W., Felitti, V. J., Dong, M., & Giles, W. H. (2005). Long-term consequences of childhood sexual abuse by gender of victim. American Journal of Preventive Medicine, 28(5), 430–438. https://doi.org/10.1016/j.amepre.2005.01.015

ECPAT International. (2020). Summary paper on sexual exploitation of children in travel and tourism. https://www.ecpat.org/wp-content/uploads/2021/05/Summary-paper-on-sexual-exploitation-of-children-in-travel-and-tourism-2020.pdf

Exploring Parenting Styles Patterns and Children's Socio-Emotional Skills. (n.d.). PMC. https://pmc.ncbi.nlm.nih.gov/articles/PMC10378631/

Felitti, V. J., Anda, R. F., Nordenberg, D., Williamson, D. F., Spitz, A. M., Edwards, V., Koss, M. P., & Marks, J. S. (1998). Relationship of childhood abuse and household dysfunction to many of the leading causes of death in adults: The Adverse Childhood Experiences (ACE) Study. American Journal of Preventive Medicine, 14(4), 245–258. https://doi.org/10.1016/S0749-3797(98)00017-8

Finkelhor, D. (2008). Childhood victimization: Violence, crime, and abuse in the lives of young people. Oxford University Press.

Finkelhor, D., Turner, H. A., Shattuck, A., & Hamby, S. L. (2014). Violence, crime, and exposure to violence among children and youth. JAMA Pediatrics, 169(8), 746-754.

First Nations Health Authority. (n.d.). Find your healing path: Support services for residential school and intergenerational survivors. https://www.fnha.ca/about/news-and-events/news/find-your-healing-path-support-services-for-residential-school-and-intergenerational-survivors

Freyd, J. J. (1996). Betrayal trauma: The logic of forgetting childhood abuse. Harvard University Press.

Goffman, E. (1963). Stigma: Notes on the management of spoiled identity. Prentice-Hall.

Government of British Columbia. (2021). Enhancing Indigenous-led wellness supports for residential school survivors. BC Gov News. https://news.gov.bc.ca/releases/2021IRR0059-001857

Government of Canada. (2021, August 10). Government of Canada enhances support to Indigenous communities to respond to and heal from the ongoing impacts of residential schools. https://www.canada.ca/en/crown-indigenous-relations-northern-affairs/news/2021/08/government-of-canada-enhances-support-to-indigenous-communities-to-respond-to-and-heal-from-the-ongoing-impacts-of-residential-schools.html

Herman, J. L. (2015). Trauma and recovery: The aftermath of violence--From domestic abuse to political terror. Basic Books.

Hershkowitz, I., Horowitz, D., & Lamb, M. E. (2007). Individual and family variables associated with disclosure and nondisclosure of child abuse in Israel. Child Maltreatment, 12(2), 166-175.

Indian Residential School Survivors Society. (n.d.). Indian residential schools. https://www.irsss.ca/indian-residential-schools

Indian Residential School Survivors Society. (n.d.). IRSSS | Indian Residential School Survivors Society. https://www.irsss.ca

Indigenous Peoples Atlas of Canada. (2018, October 22). Redress and healing.

https://indigenouspeoplesatlasofcanada.ca/article/redress-and-healing/

Indigenous Services Canada. (2020). Act respecting First Nations, Inuit and Métis children, youth and families. Government of Canada.

Indigenous Services Canada. (2024). Indigenous child and family services. Retrieved from https://www.canada.ca/en/indigenous-services-canada

Indigenous Services Canada. (n.d.). Indian Residential Schools Resolution Health Support Program. https://www.sac-isc.gc.ca/eng/1581971225188/1581971250953

Institute for Security Studies. (2018). Youth crime and community-based interventions in Africa: A comparative analysis. Cape Town: ISS Press.

IntechOpen. (2024). Traditional African medicine. https://www.intechopen.com/chapters/75561

International Labour Organization. (2017). Global estimates of modern slavery: Forced labour and forced marriage. ILO Publications.

International Rescue Committee. (2022, June 22). What Ukraine's children need amid the trauma of war. https://www.rescue.org/article/what-ukraines-children-need-amid-trauma-war

Jang, S. J., Johnson, B. R., Hays, J., Hallett, M., & Duwe, G. (2008). Faith-based approaches for controlling the delinquency of juvenile offenders. U.S. Department of Justice, Office of Justice Programs.

Jang, S. J., Johnson, B. R., Hays, J., Hallett, M., & Duwe, G. (2008). Religion and misconduct in "Angola" prison: Conversion, congregational participation, religiosity, and self-identities. Justice Quarterly, 25(2), 509-537.

Johnson, B. R. (2011). Religion: The forgotten factor in cutting youth crime and saving at-risk urban youth. Manhattan Institute for Policy Research.

Johnson, B. R. (2011). More God, less crime: Why faith matters and how it could matter more. Templeton Press.

Johnson, B. R., & Larson, D. B. (2003). The InnerChange Freedom Initiative: A preliminary evaluation of America's first faith-based prison program. Center for Research on Religion and Urban Civil Society.

Johnson, B. R., Larson, D. B., & Pitts, T. C. (2000). Religious programming, institutional adjustment, and recidivism among former inmates in Prison Fellowship programs. Justice Quarterly, 14(1), 145-166.

Kellogg, N., & Committee on Child Abuse and Neglect. (2005). The evaluation of sexual abuse in children. Pediatrics, 116(2), 506-512.

Kelmendi, K. (2013). Violent behaviour among elementary and high school students in Kosovo: Prevalence and correlates. Psychology, 4(5), 1–9. https://doi.org/10.4236/psych.2013.45074

Knight, C. (2018). Therapeutic use of self: Theoretical and evidence-based considerations for clinical practice and supervision. Clinical Supervisor, 37(2), 397-416.

Koss, M. P., & Harvey, M. R. (1991). The rape victim: Clinical and community interventions (2nd ed.). SAGE Publications.

Kübler-Ross, E. (1969). On death and dying. New York: Macmillan.

Lalor, K., & McElvaney, R. (2010). Child sexual abuse, links to later sexual exploitation/high-risk sexual behavior, and prevention/treatment programs. Trauma, Violence, & Abuse, 11(4), 159–177. https://doi.org/10.1177/1524838010378299

Little Saints Orphanages. (2024). Promoting children's rights in

Nigeria. Retrieved from organizational reports.

Lloyd, R. (2011). Girls like us: Fighting for a world where girls are not for sale. HarperCollins.

Maillet Criminal Law. (2024, May 24). Rehabilitation or retribution: Approaches to juvenile justice. https://www.mailletcriminallaw.com/blog/rehabilitation-or-retribution-approaches-to-juvenile-justice/

Maltz, W. (2012). The sexual healing journey: A guide for survivors of sexual abuse. William Morrow Paperbacks.

Martin, J. A., Hurd, N. M., & Szwedo, D. E. (2024). Co-occurring trauma- and stressor-related and substance-related disorders in youth: A narrative review. PMC. https://pmc.ncbi.nlm.nih.gov/articles/PMC11600332/

Maté, G. (2008). In the realm of hungry ghosts: Close encounters with addiction. North Atlantic Books.

McAleer Law. (2025, January 16). Rehabilitation vs. punishment: What works best for juvenile offenders? https://mcaleerlaw.net/rehabilitation-vs-punishment-what-works-best-for-juvenile-offenders/

McClelland, G. M., Elkington, K. S., Teplin, L. A., & Abram, K. M. (2004). Multiple substance use disorders in juvenile detainees. Journal of the American Academy of Child & Adolescent Psychiatry, 43(10), 1215-1224.

MedLife Movement. (2023, September 14). African medical traditions: Healing practices and cultural insights. https://www.medlifemovement.org/medlife-stories/global-topics/the-fascinating-traditions-of-healing-and-medicine-in-african-cultures/

Melhem, N. M., Moritz, G., Walker, M., Shear, M. K., & Brent, D. (2007). Phenomenology and correlates of complicated grief in children and adolescents. Journal of the American Academy of Child

& Adolescent Psychiatry, 46(4), 493-499.

Military.com. (2024, July 9). Pell Grants for Children of the Fallen (Iraq and Afghanistan Service Grants). https://www.military.com/education/money-for-school/iraq-and-afghanistan-service-grant.html

Mitchell, T. L., Arseneau, J. R., & Thomas, D. (2019). Colonial trauma: Complex, continuous, collective, cumulative and compounding effects on the mental health of Indigenous peoples in Canada and beyond. International Journal of Indigenous Health, 14(2), 74-94.

Molla, A., Sisay, B., Techane, M., Yakob, K., & Seid, E. (2024). Substance use among young people in sub-Saharan Africa: A systematic review and meta-analysis. Frontiers in Psychiatry, 15, 1328318. https://www.frontiersin.org/journals/psychiatry/articles/10.3389/fpsyt.2024.1328318/full

National Center for Biotechnology Information. (2024). Integrating spiritual and Western treatment modalities in Native American substance user centers. https://pmc.ncbi.nlm.nih.gov/articles/PMC4104509/

National Center for Biotechnology Information. (n.d.). Reentry of young offenders from the justice system: A developmental perspective. https://pmc.ncbi.nlm.nih.gov/articles/PMC2813457/

National Center for Biotechnology Information. (n.d.). The intergenerational effects of Indian Residential Schools: Implications for the concept of historical trauma. PMC. https://pmc.ncbi.nlm.nih.gov/articles/PMC4232330/

National Center for Health Statistics. (2021). Foster care statistics in the United States. U.S. Department of Health and Human Services.

National Center for Missing & Exploited Children. (2017). Online enticement of children: An in-depth analysis of CyberTipline reports.

https://www.missingkids.org/content/dam/pdfs/ncmec-analysis/Online%20Enticement%20Pre-Travel.pdf

National Center for Trauma-Informed Care. (2023). A trauma-informed guide to caring for adolescents following sexual assault. Behavioral Health Services Review.

National Center on Addiction and Substance Abuse. (2010). Criminal neglect: Substance abuse, juvenile justice and the children left behind. Columbia University.

National Child Traumatic Stress Network. (2021). Effects of complex trauma. https://www.nctsn.org/what-is-child-trauma/trauma-types/complex-trauma/effects

National Child Traumatic Stress Network. (2024). Supporting military families during deployment. Author.

National Foster Youth Institute. (2021). Foster care statistics. https://www.nfyi.org/issues/foster-care-statistics/

National Human Trafficking Hotline. (2021). National Human Trafficking Hotline data report. Polaris Project.

National Institute of Mental Health. (2021). Mental illness. https://www.nimh.nih.gov/health/statistics/mental-illness

National Institute on Drug Abuse. (2024, December 17). Reported use of most drugs among adolescents remained low in 2024. https://nida.nih.gov/news-events/news-releases/2024/12/reported-use-of-most-drugs-among-adolescents-remained-low-in-2024

Native Wellness Research Institute. (2024). A systematic review of trauma interventions in Native communities. PMC Health Disparities Journal.

Nishnawbe-Aski Legal Services. (2024, December 18). Restorative justice. https://nanlegal.on.ca/restorative-justice/

O'Hagan, K. (2006). Identifying emotional and psychological abuse: A guide for child protection. Open University Press.

Office of Justice Programs. (n.d.). Cultivating healing by implementing restorative practices for youth: Protocol for a cluster randomized trial. https://www.ojp.gov/ncjrs/virtual-library/abstracts/cultivating-healing-implementing-restorative-practices-youth

Office of Juvenile Justice and Delinquency Prevention. (n.d.). Literature review: Restorative justice for juveniles. https://ojjdp.ojp.gov/model-programs-guide/literature-reviews/restorative-justice-for-juveniles

Olsson, J. (2013). Youth violence in Sierra Leone: A restorative justice response. ResearchGate. https://www.researchgate.net/publication/258436852_Youth_Violence_in_Sierra_Leone_A_Restorative_Justice_Response

Paolucci, E. O., Genuis, M. L., & Violato, C. (2001). A meta-analysis of the published research on the effects of child sexual abuse. The Journal of Psychology, 135(1), 17-36.

Parenting Styles and Parent–Adolescent Relationships: The Mediating Roles of Behavioral Autonomy and Parental Authority. (2018, November 13). Frontiers in Psychology. https://www.frontiersin.org/journals/psychology/articles/10.3389/fpsyg.2018.02187/full

Parenting Styles: A Closer Look at a Well-Known Concept. (2018). Journal of Child and Family Studies. https://link.springer.com/article/10.1007/s10826-018-1242-x

Perry, B. D. (2009). Examining child maltreatment through a neurodevelopmental lens: Clinical applications of the neurosequential model of therapeutics. Journal of Loss and Trauma, 14(4), 240–255. https://doi.org/10.1080/15325020903004350

Perry, B. D., & Szalavitz, M. (2006). The boy who was raised as a dog: And other stories from a child psychiatrist's notebook. Basic Books.

Porges, S. W. (2011). The polyvagal theory: Neurophysiological foundations of emotions, attachment, communication, and self-regulation. W. W. Norton & Company.

Prevention Coalition. (n.d.). Drug use among youth: Facts & statistics. TalkHeart2Heart.org. https://talkheart2heart.org/resources/drug-use-among-youth-facts-statistics/

Pros and Cons of 4 Parenting Styles. (2025, May 20). Wellspring Prevention. https://wellspringprevention.org/blog/pros-cons-parenting-styles/

Ravi, A., & Little, M. (2017). Providing trauma-informed care. American Family Physician, 95(10), 655-661.

Reczek, R. (2024, May 19). Unpacking the epidemic of parental estrangement. Psychology Today. https://www.psychologytoday.com/us/blog/from-fear-to-intimacy/202405/unpacking-the-epidemic-of-parental-estrangement

Reczek, R., & Bosley-Smith, J. (2022). Parent–adult child estrangement in the United States by gender, race/ethnicity, and sexuality. Journal of Marriage and Family. Advance online publication. https://doi.org/10.1111/jomf.12985

ReliefWeb. (n.d.). Humanitarian Action for Children 2024 - Ukraine and Refugee Response. https://reliefweb.int/report/ukraine/humanitarian-action-children-2024-ukraine-and-refugee-response

Rodaughan, J., Murrup-Stewart, C., & Berger, E. (2024). Aboriginal practitioners' perspectives on culturally informed practice for trauma healing in Australia. Child Abuse & Neglect, 45(3), 211-225.

Rothschild, B. (2000). The body remembers: The psychophysiology of trauma and trauma treatment. W. W. Norton & Company.

Salter, A. C. (2003). Predators: Pedophiles, rapists, and other sex offenders. Basic Books.
Save the Children. (n.d.). Ukraine refugees: How to help. https://www.savethechildren.org/us/what-we-do/emergency-response/refugee-children-crisis/ukrainian-refugees

Save the Children UK. (2024). Scattered and vulnerable: children in Ukraine two years into war. https://www.savethechildren.org.uk/blogs/2024/children-in-ukraine-two-years-into-war

Schwandt, M. L., Heilig, M., Hommer, D. W., George, D. T., & Ramchandani, V. A. (2013). Childhood trauma exposure and alcohol dependence severity in adulthood: Mediation by emotional abuse severity and neuroticism. Alcoholism: Clinical and Experimental Research, 37(6), 984-992.

Schweitzer & Davidian. (n.d.). Rehabilitation vs. incarceration: What works best for juvenile offenders in California? https://www.avoidjail.net/blog/2023/july/rehabilitation-vs-incarceration-what-works-best-/

Shackford-Bradley, J., & Nibo, J. (2019). Addressing male youth violence in Nigeria through restorative justice. Academia.edu. https://www.academia.edu/38078176/Addressing_Male_Youth_Violence_in_Nigeria_through_Restorative_Justice

Shange, S., & Ross, E. (2022). Prayer to the ancestral spirits, sacrificial rituals and music in African spirituality. Journal of Social Science Research. https://scielo.org.za/scielo.php?script=sci_arttext&pid=S0037-80542020000400004

Shared Hope International. (2018). National report on domestic minor sex trafficking: America's prostituted children. https://sharedhope.org/wp-content/uploads/2018/08/SHI_National_Report_2018_Final.pdf

Siegel, D. J. (2012). The developing mind: How relationships and the brain interact to shape who we are. Guilford Press.

Sinclair, S. (2022). Traditional indigenous healing approaches for foster youth. Journal of Indigenous Mental Health, 15(3), 45-62.

Smallwood, R., Woods, C., Power, T., & Usher, K. (2021). Understanding the impact of historical trauma due to colonization on the health and well-being of Indigenous young peoples: A systematic scoping review. International Journal of Environmental Research and Public Health, 18(4), 1462.

Statistics Canada. (2016). Census data on Indigenous children in care. Government of Canada.

Substance Abuse and Mental Health Services Administration. (2014). Trauma-informed care in behavioral services. Treatment Improvement Protocol (TIP) Series 57. HHS Publication No. (SMA) 13-4801.

Substance Abuse and Mental Health Services Administration. (2019). Screening and assessment of co-occurring disorders in the justice system. Treatment Improvement Protocol (TIP) Series 57. HHS Publication No. (SMA) 13-4017.

Substance Abuse and Mental Health Services Administration. (2020). Key substance use and mental health indicators in the United States: Results from the 2019 National Survey on Drug Use and Health. Center for Behavioral Health Statistics and Quality.

Substance Abuse and Mental Health Services Administration. (2024). Family therapy can help: For people in recovery from mental illness or addiction. https://www.samhsa.gov/find-help/national-helpline

The Annie E. Casey Foundation. (2024, August 9). What is restorative justice in the juvenile justice system? https://www.aecf.org/blog/what-is-restorative-justice-for-young-people

The authoritative parenting style: An evidence-based guide. (2024, April 25). Parenting Science. https://parentingscience.com/authoritative-parenting-style/

The Dandelion Philosophy. (2024). Afrocentric approaches to healing intergenerational trauma. Community Psychology Practice.

The power of authoritative parenting: A cross-national study of effects of exposure to different parenting styles on life satisfaction. (2020, July 23). ScienceDirect. https://www.sciencedirect.com/science/article/abs/pii/S0190740920300918X

Traditional Medicine and Healing. (2024). Understanding traditional African healing. PMC. https://www.ncbi.nlm.nih.gov/pmc/articles/PMC4651463/

Trafficking Victims Protection Act of 2000, Pub. L. No. 106-386, 114 Stat. 1464.

Types of Parenting Styles and Effects on Children. (n.d.). StatPearls - NCBI Bookshelf. https://www.ncbi.nlm.nih.gov/books/NBK568743/

UK Government. (2024, November 11). Country policy and information note: Unaccompanied children, Afghanistan. https://www.gov.uk/government/publications/afghanistan-country-policy-and-information-notes/country-policy-and-information-note-unaccompanied-children-afghanistan-november-2024-accessible

UN Women. (2021). Facts and figures: Ending violence against women. https://www.unwomen.org/en/what-we-do/ending-violence-against-women/facts-and-figures

UNICEF. (2024). Delivering for the children of Afghanistan. https://www.unicef.org/emergencies/delivering-support-afghanistans-children

UNICEF. (2024, May 22). UNICEF addressing child trauma and displacement in Ukraine's Kharkiv. UN News.

https://news.un.org/en/interview/2024/05/1150111

UNICEF. (n.d.). Guidance for protecting displaced and refugee children in and outside of Ukraine. https://www.unicef.org/emergencies/guidance-protecting-displaced-children-ukraine

UNICEF Nigeria. (2023). Alternative care for vulnerable children in Nigeria. UNICEF Country Office.

United Nations Office for the Coordination of Humanitarian Affairs. (2024). Afghanistan Humanitarian Needs and Response Plan 2025. https://www.unocha.org/publications/report/afghanistan/afghanistan-humanitarian-needs-and-response-plan-2025-december-2024

United Nations Office on Drugs and Crime. (2015). Comprehensive study on youth crime in Africa. Vienna: UNODC.

United Nations Office on Drugs and Crime. (2021). Global report on trafficking in persons 2020. United Nations Publications.

U.S. Committee for Refugees and Immigrants. (2024, October 30). Ukrainian refugee support: October 2024 aid and relief updates. Refugees.org. https://refugees.org/ukraine-october-2024/

U.S. Department of Health and Human Services. (2023). The AFCARS Report: Foster care statistics. Administration for Children and Families.

Van der Kolk, B. A. (2014). The body keeps the score: Brain, mind, and body in the healing of trauma. Viking.

Victims of Trafficking and Violence Protection Act of 2000, Pub. L. No. 106-386, 114 Stat. 1464.

Vienna Psychological Group. (2023). Historical perspectives on juvenile justice. Academic Press.

Vienna Psychological Group. (2023, June 28). History of the juvenile delinquency system. Retrieved from https://www.viennapsychologicalgroup.com/history-of-the-juvenile-delinquency-system/

Vkeel Legal Blog. (2022). Evolution of juvenile justice systems: A comparative analysis. Legal Academic Publishers.

Vkeel Legal Blog. (2022). Juvenile delinquency: From ancient to modern times. Retrieved from https://www.vkeel.com/legal-blog/juvenile-delinquency-from-ancient-to-modern-times

Webb, J. (2012). Running on empty: Overcome your childhood emotional neglect. Morgan James Publishing.

Which Parenting Style Is Best? (2024, November 4). Nurtured First. https://nurturedfirst.com/baby/best-parenting-style/

Williamson, C., & Prior, M. (2009). Domestic minor sex trafficking: A network of underground players in the Midwest. Journal of Child and Adolescent Trauma, 2(1), 46-61.

Wilson College. (2024, January 3). Juvenile justice: Rehabilitation vs. disciplinary action. https://online.wilson.edu/resources/juvenile-justice-rehabilitation-vs-disciplinary-action/

Wolfelt, A. D. (2004). When children grieve: For adults to help children deal with death, divorce, pet loss, moving, and other losses. Companion Press.

World Health Organization. (2017). Responding to children and adolescents who have been sexually abused: WHO clinical guidelines. https://www.who.int/publications/i/item/9789241550147

World Health Organization. (2021). Global status report on preventing violence against children 2020. https://www.who.int/publications/i/item/9789240004191

World Health Organization. (2021). Disability and health. https://www.who.int/news-room/fact-sheets/detail/disability-and-health

World Health Organization Europe. (2024, April 25). Alcohol, e-cigarettes, cannabis: concerning trends in adolescent substance use, shows new WHO/Europe report. https://www.who.int/europe/news/item/25-04-2024-alcohol--e-cigarettes--cannabis--concerning-trends-in-adolescent-substance-use--shows-new-who-europe-report

World Health Organization (WHO). (2002). World Report on Violence and Health. Geneva: WHO.

World Vision. (2025, January 15). Ukraine crisis: Facts, FAQs, and how to help. https://www.worldvision.org/disaster-relief-news-stories/ukraine-crisis-facts-faqs-and-how-to-help

Yellowhead Institute. (2022, January 22). Let's talk about Indigenous mental health: Trauma, suicide & settler colonialism. https://yellowheadinstitute.org/2022/01/22/lets-talk-about-indigenous-mental-health-trauma-suicide-settler-colonialism/

Young People In Recovery. (2022). YPR mission statement. https://youngpeopleinrecovery.org/

Youth.gov. (n.d.). Substance use/misuse. https://youth.gov/youth-topics/substance-abuse

www.ingramcontent.com/pod-product-compliance
Lightning Source LLC
Chambersburg PA
CBHW050841040426
42333CB00058B/173